Tracy G
The DIO Years
&
Beyond The Skull

Jeff Westlake

ISBN:0615621147
ISBN-13:9780615621142

DEDICATION

This book is dedicated to "G" fans all around the world and to the Mighty "G" family who are a rare bunch but a perfect model of what all families should be like in support of one another.

CONTENTS

ACKNOWLEDGMENTS
Book Edited by Dave Lavender for Lavender publishing
Book Layout by Robin and Terry Kimball
Content Contributions by Jim "Big Jim" Hoelfelt, Shawn Caro,
Momma and Poppa G, Charles Bowen, Willie Fyffe, Tapio Keihanen
& Dio.net, Suzy Chavez, Alex Richter, Julie Westlake and of course,
Tracy G Grijalva.

THE INVOLVED

So that you better understand who all was involved and how they were involved here's a reference section you can use when needed. Kind of a who's who and what's what guide.

TRACY "G" GRIJALVA - The center of attention of this book. Guitar player, producer and songwriter.

Mom And Dad (Parents) - tracy G's mom and Dad. The people who created the master.

RONNIE JAMES DIO - The best vocalist heavy rock has ever seen. Platinum-selling artist who fronted Elf, Rainbow, BLack Sabbath, Heaven and Hell and Dio.

VINNY APPICE - The groove master and thunder drummer for Dio, Black Sabbath and Heaven and Hell, and many others.

JIMMY BAIN - Bass player with RJD in Rainbow and Dio.

JEFF PILSON - Bass player on the "Strange Highways" and "Angry Machine" releases and also bass player in Dokken and Foreigner.

JERRY BEST - Bass player in Freak of Nature who opened up for Dio on the "Strange Highways" European tour in 1993. got the Dio gig in 1995 for a short period.

LARRY DENNISON - Bass player in Dio during the "Angry Machines" and the "To Hull and Back" tours.

MIKE FRASER - Producer of the "Strange Highways" release in 1993.

RUMBO STUDIO's - The studio "Strange Highways" was recorded in Los Angeles, California.

G FACTORY - Tracy G's studio.

MAN KIND - The band Tracy was in when he got the Dio gig.

DOKKEN - Los Angeles area rock band that was the first band to make a mark with Jeff Pilson in it.

WYN DAVIS - Producer and engineer. Wyn was the Engineer on the "Angry Machines" release and the mixing engineer for the live "Inferno: Last in Live" release.

KARL SANDOVAL - Guitar builder for many well known players throughout the years to include Tracy and Randy Rhoads.

DAVE CERVANTES - Guitar builder for Tracy .

VINNIE MOORE - Well known and respected guitar player who is currently with U.F.O.and was in the auditions for "Strange Highways."

PHIL MOGG - Lead vocalist of U.F.O.

PETE WAY - Bass player for U.F.O. and Waysted as well as producer

U.F.O. - British Hard Rock band that broke into the mainstream in the late 70's and early 80's. Best known for being the band that introduced Michael Schenker to the world.

MICHAEL SCHENKER - Guitar player for U.F.O., M.S.G. and the Scorpions who was mentioned in the tryout portion of Dio getting back together to Tracy while the auditions were going on.

YNGWIE MALMSTEEN - Neoclassical guitar player that came into the public conscience in the early 80's as the guitar player in Alcatrazz. He was also mentioned as a player in the audition process for Dio.

WENDY DIO - Manager and former wife to Ronnie James Dio.

PARENTS - Tracy G parents.

RITCHIE BLACKMORE - Guitarist in Deep Purple and later in Rainbow with Ronnie James Dio and an influence to Tracy growing up.

JEFF BECK - English born guitarist that was also a big influence on Tracy growing up.

TONY IOMMI - Guitar master in Black Sabbath and Heaven and Hell. Played with Ronnie James Dio and is responsible for G loving the heavy stuff.

JAMES KOTTAK - Drummer for the Scorpions and Kingdom Come who filled in for Vinny Appice during a sickness on the "Angry Machines" tour.

SIMON WRIGHT - Drummer for Dio and AC/DC

SCOTT WARREN - Keyboard player in Dio and Heaven and Hell.

ROWAN ROBERTSON - Guitar player for Dio's "Lock up the Wolves" release in 1990.

"STRANGE HIGHWAYS" - 1993/1994 Warner Brother/Reprise release of the Dio band.

"ANGRY MACHINES" - 1996 Mayhem Records release of the Dio band.

"INFERNO THE LAST IN LIVE" - 1998 Mayhem Records live release of the Dio band

IGOR - Tracy's pedal board that was given its name by Mr. Dio himself.

HOLY GUITAR - The original unique guitar that was built by Karl Sandoval for Tracy.

GEEZER BUTLER - Bass player with Ronnie James Dio in Black Sabbath and Heaven and Hell.

CARL SENTENCE - Singer in Geezer Butler's band in 1991.

DRIVEN - The first post Dio project for G.

GOAD-ED - Post-Dio band that Tracy formed with ex-Dio bassist Larry Dennison and Korn Drummer Ray Luzier

RAY LUZIER - Drummer for Driven and Goad-ed as well as Korn.

TIM SAXTON - Vocalist in Driven

JASON WITTE - Vocalist in Goad-ed.

THE REASON

I have spent my entire life with music. Not just listening but playing, recording and producing. Ever since I was old enough to hold a guitar it has engulfed everything about me.

Growing up I was influenced by my grandparents and their love of country music. Johnny Cash, Hank Williams, Glen Campbell, Chet Atkins were the things I heard on a daily basis for the first 5 years of my life. I can remember "The Grand Ole Opry" and "Hee Haw" as being staples in the family's life every week. On Tuesdays at 8 p.m. we watched "The Johnny Cash Show" as that was my show when I was a kid.

At age six I was turned on to something much more alive than what I had been used to at that point. In crashing through the walls came the likes of Black Sabbath and Deep Purple courtesy of my oldest sister Terri. I can still remember hearing that stuff like it was yesterday. So as the years went on I still held on to Johhny Cash and my earliest music but I was slowly changing over to the rock side and more importantly the sounds of electric guitar with distortion.

By the time I had turned 12 I was becoming aware of Kiss, Rush and Ronnie James Dio. Rainbow was the word of the times for me along with Kiss. Through all of my teen years I was always on the hunt for new bands and new guitar players making me the go to guy in our school when people wanted to know anything about the current state of music. During that entire time while I was always looking for the new player and band I always kept going back to one person no matter what band he was in and that was DIO. By the time I turned 18

Ronnie James Dio had been through Rainbow, Sabbath and now he was into his own band DIO.

Through the years I had loved and still do love Tony Iommi and his great riffs. I also developed a taste for Michael Schenker, early Ace Frehley, Jake E. Lee, Dave Meniketti, Ricky Medlock and a stable of other guys as well. I remember these guys building my life brick by brick as I grew up. The great thing about all of these players was how different they all were from each other.

I would spend all of my spare time playing and figuring out the licks and the tricks of all of these guitar gods. I never copied them because I felt that was a waste of time and I wanted to stand on my own as well as a player. It was, however, an education to study what they did and then to see them live and see how they did the cool licks. It was like an in-person lesson from a private teacher. I spent a lot of money on that education but I do not know that I ever have spent money any better.

Although I was being molded by the metal, I felt like around the late 80's things got really stale and too predictable. Buying a record by a new band was still cool at the time but they all were starting to sound the same with the same licks and the same pattern of writing songs that just left ya feeling like it was robotic in nature. There was nothing new happening in the scene. The hair was getting bigger but the sounds, ideas, technique and over all playing and songs were just not there like it was in the early 80's.

There were still bands out there I liked putting out records but for me it was just not with the same edge or ferocity. So from the late 80's until 1993 it was like nothing changed or the feeling of living in the 20's or 30's when music all sounded the same. There were no new licks, no new styles and no new energy. Not to say there were no good products but none that had a newness to them that you said wow over.

Ronnie was back with Sabbath in 1992 and that was great for me. They put out a great modern record that had really great songs but the production was too light for a Sabbath release. It was all vocals and drums it seemed without enough power like the "Mob Rules" release had been in 1981. I did however see that tour several times and loved every minute of it. I was feeling a new lease on life with that but then they broke up yet again. This was bad but great all at the same time. It was one of those times I was cussing but did not know what was around the corner.

So we are back to the crap again and the band of the day being Guns N' Roses. I guess I was supposed to be happy about that but I was far from it. Again just many of the same licks on guitar thrown under a slightly different melody. It was like people were saying watch me play the lick I learned on my tenth lesson and just kept on abusing that one lick. Hello; there is so much more to the guitar than the blues licks your grandpa taught you. This feeling went on for what seemed to be an eternity.

Then it finally happened. That sound I was looking and waiting on for years. I had always loved Iommi for his awesome riffs and thick tone. However at one point it just stopped growing. Through the 80's after Dio left Sabbath, Tony struggled with his sound and vibe as well and that was hard for an Iommi fan to deal with to be honest. Then in 1993 I was introduced to Tracy G through the Dio "Strange Highways" release. It was fresh, bigger than life, had attitude and was not the same old crap thrown in a blender. That CD just literally slapped the taste right out of my mouth from the first notes to the last one in the 11 songs on that disc. I could not believe I was hearing what was on there when I first listened to it. It took me 15 minutes to just get past the opening riff of "Jesus, Mary and the Holy Ghost." I kept rewinding it on my CD player to just hear that. At that moment and until this day that CD had a huge impact on me not only as a guitar player and musician but as a DIO fan as well. That is the absolute quintessential release of his career. It was fresh, bold and oozing with attitude for the entire length of the CD.

Why was it that way I kept asking. Appice is the same, Jeff Pilson is new but who is the Tracy G dude? I studied the CD intensely for many months if not years actually. The CD just had a vibe about it that was so brutal and so angry but with the coolest sounds and arrangements I could ever remember hearing. I finally figured out after a while that those cool sounds were coming from the guitar. I then went and saw DIO live in Milwaukee at Summerfest. Holy shit was that unreal. I watched the guitar player all night and what he brought to the stage and the band with amazement. What in the hell was at that guy's feet to do all of this stuff. He was like a mad scientist up there with all the buttons in his pedal board and he was a master technician with it.

The sounds were cool all unto themselves but man what a player. His rhythm playing was Iommi on steroids and his leads were fresh takes on what had since become stale and boring years before. All of the sudden Dio classics be it his own, Sabbath or Rainbow had a new spin and a new life to them and I for one was ever happy about that. It was amazing to see the stuff they had pulled off on the "Strange Highways" CD was exactly the same live. Not meaning it was a copy but that the intensity and the playing matched what that CD brought to the listener. I have never heard Ronnie sound better and the band at that show and on that product was on fire. Smiles galore on that stage that night and every show of that tour that I was lucky enough to see. No two nights ever felt the same and the set list would change here and there a bit but the freshness was apparent every show.

The band went on to record one more studio product and one live opus as well. While "Angry Machines" was not quite the same as it's predecessor it was still a great record and better than many of the Dio CD's that came before it. The live CD was brilliant and I loved the bonus tracks for the Japan release as they were two blistering versions of Sabbath tunes.

Generally 1993 through 1999 was Dio's most creative period and that was largely due to Tracy G and the brilliance this man brought to the band with his playing. He was not from the school of square box thinkers but was rather from the forward-looking and thinking department.

There are some who did not like Tracy and his playing. Those people go in the square box. These are the people who get a job, have 2.5 kids, live in a house in a neighborhood that the only difference is the house number; otherwise they all look the same. They pay taxes, retire after working for the man and never have an identity only to die regretful and bored.

Then there are those who loved Tracy's playing and what he brought not only to DIO but to the musical world itself. Those people never have mold or moss on their feet. They may still have 2.5 kids and a house and neighbors but there world is colored slightly different and with purpose. See those folks don't accept the same old same old because that is the way it has always been. Why dare to be different because you might upset the norm or the close friends who all are in the square box.

Thank God for Tracy and his brilliance and him sticking to his guns and not being a puppet for any one. In this book we are going to discover his time while in DIO as the longest tenured guitarist in one stretch in the history of the band. We are going to go behind how he felt and what it was like for him from getting the gig to leaving the gig and all the stuff in between just like an Oreo.

This is G the DIO years....how he felt, reacted and the music he made. This is the most underrated guitar player of our time who continues to make some of the best music today and because of that and the effect he had on me I have spent countless hours with him to uncover this time and bring it to you to read.

Here is the story of Tracy G, one of the best to ever strap on a guitar.

THE CALL

The year was 1993. The European Community eliminates trade barriers and creates a European single market, The State of Washington executes Westley Allan Dodd by hanging (the first legal hanging in America since 1965); $7.4 million USD is stolen from Brinks Armored Car Depot in Rochester, New York in the Fifth largest robbery in U.S. history. Four men, Samuel Millar, Father Patrick Moloney, former Rochester Police officer Thomas O'Connor, and Charles McCormick, all of whom have ties to the Provisional Irish Republican Army, are accused; IBM announces a $4.97 billion loss for 1992, the largest single-year corporate loss in United States history to date; A ferry sinks in Haiti killing approximately 1,215 out of 1,500 passengers; Bureau of Alcohol, Tobacco and Firearms agents raid the Branch Davidian compound in Waco, Texas, with a warrant to arrest leader David Koresh on federal firearms violations. Four agents and five Davidians die in the raid and a 51-day standoff begins; Authorities announce the capture of suspected World Trade Center bombing conspirator Mohammad Salameh, large protests erupt against Slobodan Milošević's regime in Belgrade; and opposition leader Vuk Drašković and his wife Danica are arrested and Israel and the Vatican establish diplomatic relations.

Besides to upheaval around the globe, 1993 was also a year in which he lost such talents as Frank Zappa, River Phoenix, Vincent Price, Arthur Ashe, Audrey Hepburn and Dizzy Gillespie.

In the metal and music world of 1993, the tectonic plates of chaos were also shifting and grinding. Rob Halford of Judas Priest leaves the band to start his own project Fight, Bruce Dickinson leaves Iron Maiden. Wolfsbane's singer Blaze Bayley is chosen to replace him, Accept reforms with Udo Dirkshneider on vocals for a new album and European/American tour.

What did the metal world gain in 1993 you ask? In a not-so-quiet corner of the world a storm was brewing and it was not far from eruption. A young California guitar wizard, Tracy Grijalva, who was not the normal I-will-see-your-pentatonic-and-raise-you-arpeggios-in-the-key-of-E axe slinger was waiting for his time with his own style. No not this guy. He could do that; but he was more interested in taking the normal everyday guitar and twisting it into his own little electrifying ball of tricks, noises and sounds to create fresh new music. He also could run solo's around your head if that is indeed what he was in the mood for.

Along with that arsenal he also had a keen sense of groove and how to lay down a riff and a groove in the same song to create not only power but emotion and leave it open for vocal interpretation. His looks may have been of the time, but his attitude, drive, equipment and over all perspective of things was - and still is - all his own.

The spring of 1993 has Tracy focused on his new band Mankind. They have been rehearsing to get out and play live in the region. As always when in this process there are so many things to look at and things to evaluate in this process. Focus is not something you struggle to gain but rather something you have to try to force yourself away from to rest. Tracy is no different from anyone in this position and maybe even more so than the normal guy or gal trying to get a band off the ground.

One afternoon in the spring of 1993 Tracy gets a call from a guy he had recorded an album with and did some touring with as well back in 1990. Vinny Appice had given Tracy a ring on the phone and asked him if he would like a try out for Dio. Well, are you fucking kidding Vinny? Just a couple months before Tracy had seen an ad in the paper saying that Dio had reformed and was looking for a guitar player to accompany Dio, Appice and Bain. G never thought in a million years he would get a call for this spot even though he had a history with the rhythm section of Dio just two short years before. In private however G had hoped Vinny would bring up his name to Ronnie but in no way expected it.

So Tracy shows up at the address given to him at a practice space rented by Dio. He got there unloaded his truck with all of his gear which was not the standard looking gear. It was all name brand stuff of the day it just had the "G" look to it.

On this day it seemed to easy but hard all at the same time. Why did it seem easy? Tracy had played with these cats before and they knew each other really well. There was no play this song or that song from Ronnie's past it was just a one-hour jam session that consisted of things they had played in the past together and some new riffs Tracy broke out just to jam on. Now why was it tough? It was tough because the master sat in the corner of the room with no real talking from him just intent listening. Occasionally leaving the room to play pinball but then to come right back in to continue listening. G however felt very good about what had taken place during that hour with Appice and Bain.

At the end of the session G learned that they were talking about having some heavy hitters like Michael Schenker to possibly try out and Vinny Moore was to come in the day after. Tracy left liking the experience and getting to meet

Ronnie but thought to himself that there was not much of a chance especially with the names they were throwing around.

So Tracy just went about business as usual and did not mention anything about the try out to his band at all. He did tell his family as they are a very tight unit unit but that was it. So it was business as usual for G and his band Man Kind and their upcoming first show and rehearsals.

About a month later the second call came. This call was even more of a shock than the first one. Let's be honest, it is one thing to get a call initially but all together different once you know the likes of the competition you were up against. Malmsteen, Moore, Schenker and the list went on.

So when the phone rang for the second time it again was Vinny on the other end. "Hey Tracy, Ronnie has narrowed the playing field to just a few guys and you are one of them. Be back at the rehearsal place at this time for another jam." To G this was a shock but also a bit of an omen. To be part of the final draw so to speak speaks volumes. So for thinking that his style was too different for Dio and that he was happy to have had the chance to try out now took a new dimension. Now it seemed hope was shining through a dusty window in a very big way.

So once again it was pack the truck up with the G gear and head back. Once there it was set up, talk a bit with the guys and then start the process again of jamming. This time however things changed.The last time with these guys it was all about the jamming together and finding the groove. This time however Ronnie had hooked up a mic and was involved in this process physically and not just with his ears.

So as Tracy and the band jammed on riffs Ronnie would pick out something he dug and would ad lib over it. Occasionally - as he always did - he would leave the room while the band was jamming on something he liked to go to his focus place; the pinball machine. Once he had something a little concrete he would come back in and have the band start over at a certain place and try his idea out. Just as quickly though he would leave again prompting Tracy to ask Vinny if something was wrong or should he change the riff. Vinny simply replied to G that Ronnie worked in that manner and that everything was OK. We all have our own way of doing things and for Ronnie it was pinball to free his mind a bit.

Again at the end of about an hour it was over. This time however, Tracy was a bit jacked on adrenaline and approached Ronnie. "So what do you think?" Ronnie looked at him and said he dug it and liked his playing but would not offer any more than that. He did go on to say that the process was not over and that Warner Brothers had a list of people they wanted him to look at as well. So again it was pack it all up and go back wondering what was going on. This was quite easily the hardest thing Grijalva had been through in his life. It was such an honor to get to play with Ronnie James Dio but at the same time the not knowing was enough to eat him alive.

In the mean time Tracy had a gig to get ready for with his band Mankind so he jumped into that to keep his mind busy. A couple weeks go by of working but in private wondering about the outcome of the biggest gig ever in his life. Would he or wouldn't he get that next call? So on a Thursday call number three came.

"Hello" answered Tracy. "Hey man how ya doing?" said Vinny Appice on the other end. "Doing great man and you?" "Well go tell your dad you got the gig man" said Appice. The funny thing about this is that even though G had been told he had the gig his first reaction was to ask how? "What happened with Moore and Malmsteen and all those other cats?" he asked. The reply was short and swift again that he got the job and he was to be at Ronnie's house the following Wednesday. So after just a few minutes on the phone Tracy G was now the gun slinger in Dio. He got to go and tell his family of the good news but still had to keep it quiet for a couple of reasons.

Now Tracy must tell his band who has worked so hard in the past few months of what has just transpired in his life and the chance that has been given to him. Up until this point G had kept the entire thing quiet because to be honest he did not in his right mind expect to get this job. So therefore he thought why say anything and possibly disrupt something if there was no need to do so. That all changed now.

So Saturday came and the gig went off like clock work. Great show and a lot of good response from fans. Even yet Tracy said nothing to the band. He did not want to do something like that in a club full of people and he wanted to talk to every guy personally about what had happened. For Tracy it was about the relationships in the band and not just the music. When you spend time putting something together like a band the relationships are very important.

So on Sunday he got up and went to each individual band member's house and broke the news face to face which in itself is very noble and honest and let's admit it - not normal in rock 'n' roll.

He had received the thing he wanted and that was an honest approach and the human element of telling his guys who had worked hard with him that a chance of a lifetime was at his feet and he got each one of the guys' support. He was now free to go forward.

So where did this free-thinking, monster axe-slinging kid come from?

Tracy was born in Whittier, California and has two sisters. Music was not something that reached in from the outside to get Tracy. Music was right there with him every day of his life from the minute he was born. Tracy's father played drums on weekends with his uncle in a band called, The Grijalva Brothers.

When Tracy was seven, he wanted to be in Little League baseball, but soon after joining a team, he came down with a childhood illness that lasted the entire baseball season. By the time he recovered, baseball season was over, leaving Tracy in search of a different activity. His parents decided to let him take music lessons. Tracy originally wanted to play drums, but ultimately decided on guitar so that he could play in his father's band some day.

His parents went out after his decision and rented an acoustic guitar and told Tracy that if he would practice every day for three months, they would buy him one of his own. Three months later he had his first electric guitar and a small amplifier. This was just the start of what was to be something big in Tracy's life.

Tracy had a few different guitar teachers when he was a boy, but one of the most memorable is the teacher that told him and his parents, "Tracy will have a hard time playing guitar because his hands are to small." So much for paid educators. He did have some good teachers, but as a child, he mostly relied on a determination more intense than most people have as adults. His sister recalls that one day when Tracy didn't want to practice his scales, his father told him to go to his room and practice until his fingers hurt. So for the next four hours he hammered and plucked on those strings until Papa G couldn't take it anymore. "Will you stop now?" his father said, to which Tracy replied, "My fingers don't hurt yet."

Interestingly, Tracy G's musical influences vary greatly. After hearing 'Shaft' by Curtis Mayfield he bought his first Wah-wah pedal. From that point on, his box of tricks has evolved into its' own identity. Of course, you'll hear more about the legendary Igor in the Gear section of the book.

When Tracy was 13, he started playing in his father's band along with his uncle and sometimes his cousin. They played at wedding receptions, parties and lounges. Although he gained much experience, Tracy eventually grew out of his dad's band. Some people will tell you that he just grew too loud for the band. He was so loud that his uncle even had a special signal for Tracy. While on-stage, he would say "number nine" into the microphone, indicating for Tracy to Turn Down! Tracy was getting loud and wanting to be a little heavier and rowdier than their classic covers from such bands as Three Dog Night, Santana and the likes

It was around that time when Tracy came across a band called Black Sabbath. That was the sound he had been looking for. Inspired by Tony Iommie's thick, heavy guitar riffs, Tracy traded in his Telecaster for a Gibson SG. Some other early musical influences included Jeff Beck, Carlos Santana, Richie Blackmore, Jimi Hendrix, and Jimmy Page.

Over the next few years, Tracy put together many different bands. ATM, Phaze, and Riff Raff, were just a few. He also started a band called Centaur with Audie Desbrow and Jack Russell of Great White fame. He also put together Swiftkick, The Tracy G Group, Rags and Mankind. He joined bands such as Temper, Blue Rebel, and Love Hate. You could find Tracy everywhere and almost anywhere in L.A. playing clubs, venues, and even backyards. He was learning something new with each and at each gig, paying his dues and then some in those early days.

All those hours locked in his room honing his craft, and then playing with a slew of bands to meld his unique sound were now paying off.

STRANGE INDEED

So Monday and Tuesday came and went basically like any other day of his life. Wednesday came and just waking up was wrong. Why was that so? Without thinking about it Tracy knew it was day one of officially being in one of the biggest rock bands the world has known; Dio. The past five weeks had been a blur if he sat down to think about it. He had gone from forming his own new band recently and getting it to the place of playing out live to being in the guitar world driver's seat as the axe man in Dio. Granted you still have to get up just like everyone else does, you still have to do the three S's just like everyone else and put your pants on one leg at a time. With all of that in mind it did not change the fact that life now was very different in so many ways.

Tracy is about to get out of bed and go to the castle. Not just any castle either, but Ronnie James Dio's castle with the band and management for his first meeting. This is not like anything he had ever done before. Granted he had played with Vinny Appice and Jimmy Bain recently but they are not - with no disrespect - Ronnie James Dio. The master of "Mid Evil" and "Devils and Lords." The guy that made what Tracy wanted to do the "in cool thing" and one of the things that drove G to this strange, new place where he now unexpectedly sat.

Just pulling up to Ronnie's house was in itself jaw dropping. Literally a small version of a castle. It was so cool to drive up and look at this place. As if that was not enough Tracy gets out of the truck and there in the next yard is Tom Petty. In Tracy's mind he is thinking; What the fuck? He could not believe what he was seeing. Ronnie James Dio and Tom Petty

23

living next door to one another was just too much as Tracy loved Petty as well. That made the walk up the driveway to the door even more surreal and G wondered if he too was just running down a dream.

Once inside Tracy was greeted by the band, Ronnie and Wendy Dio. After a few minutes of just chatting they went and sat down for the meeting to go over the process of the newly re-formed Dio. Just as a reminder message Ronnie and Vinny had just came out of Black Sabbath run. Number two, They had just recently finished up the "Dehumanizer" album and tour just to watch it all fall apart once again right in front of them due to a lack of communication. How did such a great band seem to always self destruct like this not once but twice you wonder? Tracy didn't know but he knew it now gave him a chance to work with the best singer of his time and make his own mark.

At the meeting Wendy laid out the plans for touring and as to when and where it would start. Greece was the first country on the European tour that crisscrossed that continent. As she talked of the itinerary Tracy had already lost what she had said because he was sitting there in his mind going .... "We are going to start in Greece and then go where and holy shit are you kidding me?" The longer this went on the more Tracy felt like that a pinch was not going to do. He might have to go throw himself in front of a bus to make sure it was all real because everything was just a bit too much to take in all at once. In Dio, at Ronnie's house, talking touring and making an album. All of this from just a week before playing gig number one with his own band Mankind at the top FM station in southern California.

Tracy kept quiet during the meeting until at one point he asked if he could say something. " I want to express to everyone how grateful I am for the chance to be a part of the

Dio family." Ronnie quickly cut him off and told him that he was in Dio and an equal to everyone in the band in every way and not to look at it that way. It was kind of Ronnie's way of throwing a vote of confidence G's way in front of everyone to set the tone from day one on how it was. This was something that stuck with Tracy from that day on. He was not from any point in the band treated like the new guy or a hired hand at all. He was the guitar player in Dio and that was all there was to it.

The meeting carried on with Wendy laying out the plan and finally ended with a see ya Monday around noon at the rehearsal space to start writing. Needless to say, the rest of that day was a blur as Tracy played the day over in his mind and just tried to handle the enthusiasm that was created in his head and soul from that event in itself. Monday was five very short days away at that point. The one thing G did not worry about was having material to offer. That was something he was not short on at all.

Monday came and Tracy loaded up the truck with his G Gear and went to start the process that he was so excited about. He arrived a little before starting time, got his gear and set up so that he would be ready to roll. All of the other guys showed up around the witching hour as planned. After talking a bit they proceeded to just jam on riffs and passages much like Tracy was already used to doing with these guys from a couple years before. All of that seemed to be normal to him but still that presence in the room of Dio himself was unreal to him. That was different to be sure but the outcome was to be priceless.

After about three weeks of jamming on riffs, grooves and getting some rough ideas lined out problem number one showed itself. Everyone showed up for rehearsal as normal but no Jimmy Bain. They waited a bit but not for long. Eventually, that day and for the next two weeks Ronnie, who could play everything from keyboards to trumpet and French horn, picked up an old friend, the bass, and they worked like that. So basically, Tracy and Vinny would jam a riff or a passage until Ronnie heard what he liked and then he would come in and pick up the bass. Tracy would show him what they were doing and then as a band they would work it out. This was a good two weeks as it generated "Hollywood Black" and "Pain" in that time frame. It was however not the way that worked best for Ronnie. He liked to hear the parts and start working on the melody and the arrangement and not be tied to an instrument. It was clear after two weeks that Jimmy was out and that they had to carry on and get someone else on bass.

The next Monday when the guys got to work Ronnie looked at Vinny and said, "Hey you should call Jeff Pilson and see if he has any suggestions on a player for us." Vinny and Jeff had been close for a while and who better to ask a guy who knew many people and was in the scene heavily. Vinny made a call to Jeff and the meeting had been set.

Ronnie and Vinny then took off and went to Pilson's house. Tracy stayed behind working on riffs and other songs. Sometime later that same day they showed back up with Jeff Pilson in tow. This was unexpected but so cool for Tracy to meet yet another guy he had always admired. Ronnie had told Tracy that they went to ask about players and Jeff asked Ronnie how about him. According to Tracy, Jeff was so cool and was such a high energy guy not only upon meeting him but the entire time he was in the band. Once Jeff walked into the band things just changed on a dime. Not that it was not already great but Pilson added another unique energy and chemistry to the band and to the new music that would become known as "Strange Highways." He was much more musical and could also offer cool melodies and great musical ideas as well. With Jeff you got an accomplished songwriter, a good singer, a great bass player and someone with magnetic stage presence.

Tracy came from the perspective of thick heavy guitars and not just riffs but cool beds to allow the vocals to do whatever they needed to make the song cool but still looking at everything from a groove perspective. This is something that Ronnie had not always had in the past. Granted he had worked with the absolute best in the business like Blackmore and Iommi and great players in Dio as well like Campbell, Goldy and Robertson. One thing all of those guys had in common except Iommi was that they were riff writers and you had to as a singer work over that a lot. G wanted to create great riffs but he also was equally concerned about creating the bed for the singer as well. He wanted the bed to be an open slate for Ronnie and not pigeon hole him in a riff or a pattern. This was something Iommi gave Dio as well and it worked wonderfully there. Tracy was a more modern day Iommi but also played in that heavy way that allowed Ronnie to go as dark as he wanted and that was ever obvious on this material. It was a very unusual perspective from a guitar player to create that bed for the singer of their own will. Normally the singer would hear the riff and then try to cut out a way to get over the music in their own way but G was concerned about where and how the voice would fit. This was not any voice either. He was now concerned about finding room for Dio.

Vinny helped create that with Tracy in his power playing but Pilson added another element that was also never there in the past. Ronnie and the band now had a guy who had written hit songs while in Dokken and truth be told had more rather than less to do with that band's success as well. This just all came together not only from Pilson's ideas but his playing as well which again was superior to what had been there before and something Ronnie was used to being in Sabbath. Not that Pilson was Geezer Butler but he also was not Bain and that was a good thing on many levels. He was a great player but not to the level of Butler but he brought the harmony vocals to the table which was not a big thing in any time of Sabbath but he also did not find the root note and pound it to death. Jeff Pilson had skills and he showed them in the best and most tasteful of ways.

So after the almost three-month process of writing and arranging the material for the new release Ronnie went out and brought in Canadian recording engineer Mike Frasier, who has worked with such bands as AC/DC, Metallica and Aerosmith, to produce the project. The band then moved from the smaller rehearsal room to a larger one to spread out a bit and bring Mike in to go through the material. After only two days of preproduction he said they were ready and it was off to record this thing or as Tracy said it was "time to dress the kids."

So off to the famous Rumbo Studios to record "Strange Highways." Once they got there they spent the first couple of days to the first week setting up and getting sounds for each instrument. This is a process that is always long but cool at the same time. Once in the studio so many things open up to a player that it is always a learn-something-new-all-the-time kind of thing. Once all of that work was done then it was time to record the material.

The great thing Tracy said about Frasier was that he did not try to manufacture things and attempt to get sounds that just were not there. He simply took the tones of the guitars, drums, bass and Ronnie and made sure he got the best clean recording he could. During set up and mic up Tracy said that they actually did bring in other amps and tried different sounds just to be sure but in the end everyone played with their own gear and their own unique settings for the recording. G had been in studios in the past but Rumbo, the California studio where everyone from Kiss to Roy Orbison, Tom Petty and even Spinal Tap had recorded, was the biggest and grandest of them all for him to that point. Tracy G soaked up those days drenched in the music-making process. He was there for every day of the recording of this release.

To remind everyone the year was 1993. Although technology has advanced by light years, and thousands of other metal CDs have been added to the heap since then, this release sounds as good today as anything out there now and way better than most then. It absolutely captured a hungry band honed to a razor's edge, and armed with passionate, unequalled singer boiling up with anger about many weird ways of this world. All of that emotion bleeds out onto the tape.

The band set up in the main room and tracked the CD as a live band like it was most always done back then. No click track and only sound barrier set ups between all of the players. It was in the days of do multiple takes until you got the one that just felt right at the end and then go back later and do fixes and dubs for parts that were not quite right. This way the band created a vibe that is undeniably felt in each and every song that appears on the final product.

As in most cases the drums were dealt with first followed by bass guitar, then guitar, vocals and finished off by guitar solos. It was a bit weird being in the studio laying down guitar solo's in front of a guy that had played with the world best and most known players. The funny thing that Tracy realized once the solo aspect of the recording started was that he had done little to no soloing in front of Ronnie at all. To that point the guitarist had been concerned about nothing except the beds of the songs and how tight they were. Playing a guitar solo in the writing process never ever really came into play because it was just not important. Even better was the fact that Ronnie indeed like his style and had G play a few takes on every song to be sure to capture his best. With Tracy the take before and after were always going to be different and that was one of the things that was great about his playing in this band. It was not stiff and contrived in any way and that brought a freshness that Dio the band had not seen since "Holy Diver" and "The Last in Line."

The one thing to be sure about and that was that Ronnie was on top of every aspect of this recording from the drums all the way to the guitar solo's. As Tracy said" he never missed a thing." Not only was Dio an exceptional singer but was a multi-instrumentalist who was also very sharp in every aspect of being in the industry and especially in the recording process. This translated into a very stress-free, comfortable and natural process in the studio. There were no problems or hiccups during this six-week period.

The other thing that made this process relaxing and cool for G was the fact that he stayed at the Castle during this process. It was quite a long drive from Tracy's home in Industry to Rumbo Studios so Ronnie invited G to stay with him for that time.

This was yet again an unreal experience to be able to basically share a huge home with an idol of his while recording an album with him. Ronnie told G to pick any one of the bedrooms he wanted on the homes second floor and make his self comfortable. So Tracy packed up and moved in for the recording of "Strange Highways."

"Behind the scenes and away from the reporters, cameras and industry people Ronnie was very relaxed and calm" Tracy says. "Very comfortable to be around him and he was very much a regular guy at those times." Ronnie was always doing cool things like letting Tracy watch his video library of film from the Rainbow and Sabbath days all the way to inviting G's parents to the house for a tour and just a get to know them time as Ronnie was well aware of the support that Tracy's parents gave him in his life to be a musician and succeed at what he loved.

Ronnie took the Grijalva's through the entire spotless house which he kept cleaned all on his own. He told them he once had a house keeper but had to let her go because he kept the house cleaner than she did. Then they hit the room that Tracy was occupying and he told him that he was not in any way responsible for that room as it was Tracy's mess. This was the Dio that people who met him came to know which is much different from the dragon fighting wizard that the public in general had seen for many years.

So many new and exciting things had happened to Tracy in his magical year of 1993.

To be in a studio with Vinny was old hat for Tracy. Being in the studio with Ronnie and then Jeff Pilson was not and that was the coolest thing of all. Not only was he playing and creating with the best there was in the business but he was getting paid to be there. That was almost a sin to Tracy at the time. It was just almost too hard to believe that he could get paid for this as well as be in it as a functioning part and member. That alone was the "strangest highway" of them all but G was too happy to travel on it.

The chemistry in the band was undeniable. The vibe was always upbeat and the music speaks for all of it. Big, thunderous metal on a level all its own in 1993.

DIGESTING DIO

One would think that after making a monstrous product like "Strange Highways" the band would be content and just sit back and admire the masterpiece. Well, when you are Dio that is not the case and especially since a tour had been booked well in advance. Now it was time to take the writing, recording and creative atmosphere and put it on a shelf for another time and get to the new task at hand.

The new task was getting ready for the live experience. The odd thing in all of this is that this would be the first time Tracy has played any of the old Dio stuff. He was always a fan growing up of Ronnie but was always his own player and did not do much copying or learning cover tunes after leaving his dad's band, The Grijalva Brothers.

So the first day of getting together was basically just trying to get the set list together. That alone is a big undertaking with all the big songs Ronnie had been a part of leading up to this moment. Ronnie and Vinny were the ones that did this task while Jeff and Tracy G waited to hear the final list. Tracy and Pilson were the ones behind the eight ball on this process as they will have to spend time learning the old tunes from not only Dio but Rainbow and Sabbath as well.

Tracy was even more excited to get to work on the live show as well. Tracy was always a live player and really enjoyed that part of it. Not that he did not enjoy the studio but it's a distant second to playing live. The other thing that was exciting for him was that he got to put his spin on classic tracks that Ronnie had been a part of. G knew the importance of playing the hook lines of solos and rhythm's from the standards but also wanted to inject the way he had heard those songs for years.

Growing up he was a huge fan of Blackmore and Jeff Beck who at every live show played their solos different on every occasion and that was refreshing to hear. After all if it was the same as the record why would one go to see the show and spend the money. Now Iommi pretty much played it as it was recorded as did the other Dio players. For G, that would not be the case this time around. Tracy did not intend to be predictable to anyone. To him that was a death sentence in many ways and the spontaneity of his style would prove to be very refreshing in more than just his solos.

This "Strange Highways" tour was going to be an experience that ushered in freshness on every level again for Dio. Not only was there Tracy G on guitar but there was Jeff Pilson on bass and a fresh attitude from Vinny and Ronnie as well. Gone was the stiffness of "Dream Evil" and "Lock up the Wolves." "Dream Evil" saw much turmoil in the band and led to a very stiff product. "Lock up the Wolves" saw a new kid on guitar in Rowan Robertson at the age of 17. This also led to a complete shake up in the band seeing Appice, Bain and Schnell leaving for new players. Again another stiff record with some signs of freshness on guitar but overall much of the same. Dio too was caught up in what I was not liking about music in the late 80's and early 90's. It was not just a band or two it was affecting everyone.

Much of the freshness was the guy wearing the guitar. He did not want to be anyone else, play like any one or even look like anyone. He had no conception of plodding in a gallop for an entire product now, before or ever for that matter. It takes everyone however to make that machine churn in freshness and everyone including the man in charge was firmly 100 percent in place to support that at this time. This was Dio now and it was gearing to hit you right in the balls with no apologies.

There was not a ton of cramming for the live show. You would think it would be the equivalent of studying for a finals exam in college but this was pretty simple. The set list was loaded with six tracks from the newly completed "Strange Highways," and just another 10 tracks from Ronnie's past. Amazing how excitement makes learning songs seem like nothing, not to mention learning songs from one of your idol's past.

November and December of 1993s set list for Europe was

* Intro (someone scanning through radio stations)

* "Stand Up And Shout"

* "Strange Highways"

* "Don't Talk To Strangers"

* "Evilution"

* "Hollywood Black"

* "Here's To You"

* "Children Of The Sea"

* "Holy Diver"

* "Heaven And Hell"

* "Man On The Silver Mountain"

* "Jesus Mary & The Holy Ghost"

* "Pain"

* Guitar Solo

* "Pain"

* "The Last In Line"

* "Rainbow In The Dark" (encore)

* "We Rock" (encore)

* "Mob Rules" (encore)

The dates and venues for this set list were

04.11.1993	Rodon Club	Athens	Greece
05.11.1993	Rodon Club	Athens	Greece
06.11.1993	Rodon Club	Athens	Greece
08.11.1993	Zeleste	Barcelona	Spain
09.11.1993	Kangaroo	Madrid	Spain
11.11.1993	Sala Quattro	Aviles	Spain
13.11.1993	Warndthalle	Volkingen	Germany
14.11.1993	Philipshalle	Dusseldorf	Germany
15.11.1993	Docks	Hamburg	Germany
16.11.1993	Haus Auensee	Leipzig	Germany

7718.11.1993	Freiheitshalle	Hof	Germany
19.11.1993	Neue Welt	Berlin	Germany
20.11.1993	Jurahalle	Neumarkt	Germany
22.11.1993	Halle Gartlage	Osnabruck	Germany
23.11.1993	Stadthalle	Offenbach	Germany
24.11.1993	Forum	Ludwigsburg	Germany
25.11.1993	Terminal 1	Munich	Germany
27.11.1993	Mehrzweckhalle	Birkelbach	Germany
28.11.1993	Music Hall	Hannover	Germany
30.11.1993	Dampfblaserhalle	Augsburg	Germany
01.12.1993	Volkshaus	Zurich	Switzerland
04.12.1993	Bank Austria	Zelt Vienna	Austria
05.12.1993	Kulturfabrik Neufang	Saarbrucken	Germany
06.12.1993	Muziekcentrum	Vredenburg	Utrecht
08.12.1993	Kulturhaus	Erfurt	Germany
09.12.1993	Aladin	Bremen	Germany
10.12.1993	Eiderlandhalle	Pahlem	Germany
12.12.1993	Hammersmith Apollo	London	UK

So here it is about three weeks away from kicking off the SH tour in Athens Greece. Tracy and Jeff had taken the time and learned the songs that were needed for the live show from Ronnie's back log. At this time as well Ronnie had been introduced to Scott Warren by Jeff Pilson. Dio had been looking for a keyboard player for the live show and Scott got the job. The self-taught Chicago native keyboardist would stay with Dio in the band until Ronnie's death in 2010. With some power-packed keys now onboard, the band got into rehearsals for the shows.

Rehearsals were different from what Tracy had been through in the past. In all the bands G had been in all his life rehearsals were intense and long. That was needed to be sure the band was tight and that there were no problems with the show. This however was different; totally different. Rehearsals were never even close to what he remembered in the past. As Tracy said " on this level the musicians are so good that it all falls together much easier than it ever has for me in the past."

They did not spend hours and hours going over things. " Do you think Ronnie needs to go over "Holy Diver" or "Rainbow in the Dark" every day?" Tracy went on to explain that they would only be in rehearsals a couple hours a day, basically working on certain songs a day and certain arrangements that may be new.

It was not until the last few days that Ronnie, actually started singing full on. He would sing a bit each day but the last few days it was like a show. The band also put the final set together in those last few days as well so it all came together at the very end.

G however was still amazed at the level of musicianship and how at that ultimate level that he was at now. Things were different in every aspect of what happened in a band. Not that he was complaining mind you; just in awe of how it ran. It was a business and each member of the band took it serious and it just made what you did so much easier to be inside of.

The band did feel a bit loose to Tracy going into the first shows but within a couple of shows that all changed. It was like a blink of an eye and it was like the band had been playing as a unit forever. It was like he had been in that band with those guys for a lifetime. It was very refreshing.

The other thing that it is important to note is that Ronnie totally endorsed G's lead style. This was a new and improved version of a classic band and the guitar player fit that mold to a T. Tracy fit Ronnie's vision of the new Dio with his bombastic thick heavy style that allowed Dio to be ever darker and more aggressive in his writing. Along with that came the unique soloing that G brought to the band and helped with the new lyrical content and more modern approach from Ronnie as a writer and singer. Dio the band had totally reinvented itself.

Always aware of the classic licks in the songs and the major guitar melody lines Tracy built his own style around those things in his own way. Important to note as well that Ronnie never had the first conversation with Tracy about his style as on several occasions Ronnie would comment on stuff and how it was cool. It was all part of the new and more brutal approach of the band.

It was all fresh for this band. Gone were the plodding 4/4 rhythms and the predictable things that would make the music boring to a degree. Even in the old classics Tracy was putting in fresh licks and sound bites that gave it a much needed kick in the ass. It was a shock to the system the first time you saw the show and the new approach being taken but even the system can unfortunately get used to the predictable. It did not take long however to understand that this was cool as hell and really brought Dio back to life and to that place of being an innovator in the genre and the industry once again from every possible angle.

The first leg of the tour was just over a month long but was still great for Tracy. He was getting to see the world and the overly attractive women of Europe and especially Spain made it even more than worth it. As if being in Dio, recording a great record and getting to play live around the world were not enough; the women in Spain were unreal.

They started in Athens, Greece and finished a little over a month later in the UK and then home for the holidays. It was a little over 30 days in all for the first leg but it was a lifetime of experience for G in that small window. All the other guys had experienced traveling the world in DIO, Sabbath, Dokken, Warrant, etc., but this was the first for Grijalva.

On the last date of the first leg at the Hammersmith Apollo the band also filmed for three of the cuts off of the new album for video release. The songs were "Jesus Mary and The Holy Ghost," "Hollywood Black" and "Evilution." None of the footage has ever been released and Ronnie vetoed the release due to the look of the video shot. It would be great if the public could get a look at these videos.

"Strange Highways" was released in October 1993 in Europe and Japan and did not see release in the United States and the rest of the world until January 1994. That led to some down time for the band until the spring. A good thing too as it took weeks to get the bands gear back from Europe as it was transported back to their home base of California by boat. That was something that made Tracy very uneasy to have his beloved G gear not with him and floating around the earth somewhere on a boat.

For this leg of the tour the set list changed.

* Intro

* "Jesus Mary & The Holy Ghost"

* "Strange Highways"

* "Don't Talk To Strangers"

* "Pain"

* Guitar Solo

* "Pain"

* "Mob Rules"

* "Holy Diver"

* "Heaven And Hell"

* "Man On The Silver Mountain"

* Drum Solo

* Bass Solo

* "Heaven And Hell"

* "Evilution"

* "Give Her The Gun"

* "Stand Up And Shout"

* "The Last In Line"

* "Rainbow In The Dark" (encore, all the shows)

* "Here's To You" (encore, played here only on September 24th?)

* "Long Live Rock 'N' Roll" (encore, played only on September 24th?)

* "We Rock" (encore, not on every show?)

* "Here's To You" (encore, not on every show?)

The next leg of the tour was to be in the U.S.A and it was to be an extensive one.

01.05.1994	Pecan Street Festival	Austin, TX	USA
29.05.1994	Madison Theater	Peoria, IL	USA
01.06.1994	Orbit Room	Grand Rapids, MI	USA
02.06.1994	Hara Arena	Dayton, OH	USA
03.06.1994	State Theater	Detroit, MI	USA
04.06.1994	Agora Theater	Cleveland, OH	USA
05.06.1994	Riviera Theater	Chicago, IL	USA
08.06.1994	Casino	Hampton Beach, NH	USA
09.06.1994	Beacon Theater	New York City, NY	USA
10.06.1994	Tower Theater	Upper Darby, PA	USA
11.06.1994	Stone Pony Big Top	Asbury Park, NJ	USA
12.06.1994	The Chance	Poughkeepsie, NY	USA
15.06.1994	The Sting	New Britain, CT	USA
16.06.1994	Strand Theater	Providence, RI	USA
17.06.1994	Hammerjacks	Baltimore, MD	USA

23.06.1994	Ritz Theatre	Tampa, FL	USA
24.06.1994	The Button South	Hallandale, FL	USA
25.06.1994	Musical Moon	Tallahassee, FL	USA
26.06.1994	The Masquerade	Atlanta, GA	USA
27.06.1994	La Vela Club	Panama City Beach, FL	USA
01.07.1994	Dallas City Limits	Dallas, TX	USA
03.07.1994	The Boathouse	Norfolk, VA	USA
03.07.1994	Hurricane Alley	Houston, TX	USA
07.07.1994	The Ranch Bowl	Omaha, NE	USA
08.07.1994	The Mirage	Minneapolis, MN	USA
10.07.1994	Summerfest	Milwaukee, WI	USA
14.07.1994	Odgen Theater	Denver, CO	USA
19.07.1998	Huntridge Theater	Las Vegas, NV	USA
20.07.1994	House Of Blues	Los Angeles, CA	USA
21.07.1994	Ventura Theater	Ventura, CA	USA
11.08.1994	The Roxy	Phoenix, AZ	USA
12.08.1994	The Rock	Tucson, AZ	USA
14.08.1994	The Rock	Lakewood, CA	USA
15.08.1994	The Edge	Palo Alto, CA	USA
17.08.1994	Roseland Theater	Portland, OR	USA
18.08.1994	Under The Rail	Seattle, WA	USA

20.08.1994	Bogies	Boise, ID	USA
21.08.1994	Venue unknown	Pocatello, ID	USA
22.08.1994	Venue unknown	Billings, MN	USA
23.08.1994	Fort Ram	Fort Collins, CO	USA
24.08.1994	Rack-N-Roll	Colorado Springs, CO	USA
28.08.1994	Tremors	Colleen, Co	USA
30.08.1994	Midnight Rodeo	Little Rock, AR	USA
01.09.1994	Tipitina	New Orleans, LA	USA
03.09.1994	Toy Tiger	Louisville, KY	USA
05.09.1994	McGuffy's	Dayton, OH	USA
08.09.1994	The Village Nightclub	Lancaster, PA	USA
09.09.1994	Horizontal Boogie Bar	Rochester, NY	USA
10.09.1994	Blind Melons	Buffalo, NY	USA
11.09.1994	The Lost Horizon	Syracuse, NY	USA
14.09.1994	Arizona's	Dover, DE	USA
15.09.1994	The Strand	Providence, RI	USA
16.09.1994	Birch Hill Night Club	Old Bridge, NJ	USA
17.09.1994	The Sting	New Britain, CT	USA
18.09.1994	The Malibu Club	Lido Beach, NY	USA
20.09.1994	The Silo	Reading, PA	USA
21.09.1994	The Boots Club	West Springfield, VA	USA

22.09.1994	Bogart's	Cincinnati, OH	USA
24.09.1994	Hurricane Alley	Houston, TX	USA
25.09.1994	Johnnyland Amph	Corpus Christi, TX	USA
26.09.1994	Back Room	Austin, TX	USA
28.09.1994	Zippers	Albuquerque, NM	USA
29.09.1994	The Roxy	Phoenix, AZ	USA
30.09.1994	The Rock	Tucson, AZ	USA
02.10.1994	The Edge	Palo Alto, CA	USA

The United States was a long haul for sure but a good one. Tracy got to spend time with so many people and experience so many things that it was really just a blur to him.

In one year's time he went from having to build his own band to being in Dio. He then wrote what was to become a true monster of a product in "Strange Highways." Then after that he had hit the road for a year crisscrossing Europe and the States in support of that release. Getting to experience for the first time for Tracy overseas and travel and meeting new people in foreign lands and oh yeah; getting to play his "holy" guitar all over the world for the greatest fans and with the best singer ever wasn't a bad experience either.

The Strangest Highway you could imagine lie ahead. For the next couple of months it was down time and family time. Time to rest, reflect and also to write fresh new riffs for the next release.

ANGRY CONFUSED MACHINES

The break from Dio was longer than expected by Tracy. Instead of it being a couple of months it ended up being around five to six months. That was not a problem for him though, as always G has plenty to do to keep him busy. So while the time showed itself to him he took advantage of it to work on tunes for both Dio and for his own projects on the side.

As always as has been the case since 1987, Tracy had the Tracy G band to go out and jam with. It may not be the same guys from time to time but that was OK. There were many musician friends to pull from and make the magic happen. He also had music lessons that he gave to people who wanted to learn how to play guitar as well and Tracy was the guy they looked to in his town.

Also during this time Tracy would work on riffs for the upcoming Dio project as well. This was always something he loved to do and spent a little bit of time on a daily basis trying to write things he felt Ronnie would dig. Adding to this mayhem for him was the fact that he had just had a new guitar built. He had a custom baritone Strat made by Dave Cervantes constructed with the deepest most evil sounding set up he could ever imagine. This guitar in Tracy's mind was along with Appice's drumming going to bring yet another new element to DIO. It was felt that along with the tone of Ronnie's voice and his natural angst that this low guttural sounding axe would really bring out things in the new project.

Tracy also played on and produced various projects during his down time as he has done during his entire professional career. Creative was the word of his life and however he could be involved in blending creativity with music G was going to explore.

During the entire downtime there was little contact with the other members of the band or crew. Everyone just went their own ways and did their own things, basically which was not a bad deal since they had been together for months during the "Strange Highways" period. It is always a much needed thing to have a long break from one another after a long tour or it can get ugly in a hurry with a bunch of guys who see each other all day every day for long periods of time. Finally however after months G got the call that they were ready to start on the new project.

Everything was to be different this time from the very first day. The first thing the band did was change rehearsal facilities. This required setting up the new room totally from scratch. In total DIY fashion, this had Ronnie, Vinny and Tracy going into the room and setting it up which included painting it and getting it ready for the band to live in for a long time that no one anticipated when they started the project.

After the room was made livable they then went and got the P.A. and the equipment and spent a couple days getting that into the facility and then a couple more getting it all set up and ready to use for writing and rehearsing.The things that no one thinks about outside of the musicians. It is commonly thought that the musicians just show up and play and record and leave. The Dio band did it all including the set up.

With that done now came phase two: a new bass player. During this period of the band there were some amazingly questionable things that happened on a fairly often basis. Bass players seemed to be the main thing this was centered on. There was not only Jeff Pilson, who played on what was to become known as "Angry Machines" and Larry Dennison, who came in to play the bulk of the "Angry Machine" dates and the live release, but there was also others who tried out during this period.

One of those to do so was Rowan Robertson. The one-time British-born guitar prodigy of the "Lock up the Wolves" era was brought in by Ronnie after his asking Tracy if it was OK to do so. Tracy had received a phone call from Ronnie asking him if he would have a problem if he brought Rowan in to play bass. Tracy, of course, said cool and so it was set up. G said that Rowan, who currently plays with the band DC4, was extremely cool and a very nice person to be around and jam with.

One of the first guy to get the call in this new project was former Freak of Nature bassist Jerry Best. The band had become familiar with Best during their European run on the "Strange Highways" tour in 1993 as FON had been the main support act for that run of dates. Jerry was given the job and entered the band in the spring of 1995 and would be there for nine months.

This was the second thing that was different to G and the band. Tracy liked Jerry and thought he was a good player but it was not the same as when he had Pilson to bounce off of, A vibe is something that is very important among band members to not only the product that comes out but also how they play the material. Pilson when he arrived 3 weeks into the Highways sessions was that guy. He was the missing piece in the band and the creative process. With him gone it just was not the same as it had been nor as it needed to be in G's mind.

Once Jerry was in place it was time for the process to begin. The very first thing that was done was Ronnie giving the guys the plan for the record. Gone was Mike Fraser who produced "Strange Highways." In as producer was Ronnie James Dio. Gone was Rumbo Studios in Los Angeles and in was Total Access in Redondo Beach. The thing that facilitated this entire change had to be the move from the deep pockets of Warner Brothers Records to the new upstart Mayhem Records. This was never a discussion between G and anyone as to what label etc as he really did not care about that. Looking back however on the situation and knowing now what he knows, it was a big contributor to the changes that took place right off the bat in his mind.

The next thing was Ronnie telling everyone they were going to dry up the production of this next product and make it sound more like "Holy Diver." He also told G that he wanted him to go away from the big stereo mix and big guitar sound and go down to the single cabinet mono sound for this record. Tracy agreed with him but that does not mean in any way that he liked it at all. G has spent his life creating with care this monstrous sound he had and it was tough to bite that bullet but he did it anyway without an argument. That included the fact that they were going to cut down solos because everyone was doing it. For a guy who liked to play that was not good news but again Tracy did not argue with the new direction.

The musical movement of the 90's was one that was drastically different from the way music was approached in the 70's and 80's. Guitar solos were being replaced by just simple jam sections that Nirvana made famous for the time. The lyrical content was a swamp of negative and doom versus the upbeat, party and enjoy-life type of lyrics from previous times. This wave was enormous in the way and swiftness with which it took over. It was not a gradual thing in any way. One day it was music as normal (which does not mean good either) and the next it was this thing called Grunge.

It was so brutal in its take over that it was causing bands like Metallica, Dio and others to rethink their approach. Some seminal metal makers went almost underground, such as Dio, Scorpions, Priest and Iron Maiden, while some others survived like Metallica and a few others, but all were affected none the less.

After all the flurry of changes and activity was over it was time to get down to business. So after thee weeks of cleaning, painting, moving and getting a new bass player in it was finally time to do what they were there to do; play. So right away Tracy brought the new axe in for Ronnie to hear. It didn't go over however like Tracy was anticipating it to go. Ronnie just did not get what G was shooting for with this guitar. He went on to explain his thoughts but it was just not received as he had hoped. The experiment was to be thrown out but that guitar would see its day on this product even if it was never released. "This is Your Life" was written and originally played on that unique guitar but was later stripped and exchanged for piano. However, the original version can be heard now on YouTube.

So then the band got to jamming on riffs and ideas. Something just was not clicking like the last time. They would get ideas and Ronnie would latch onto one and they would work this idea for a couple of weeks only to scrap it at the end. Tracy and Vinny were actually liking these new ideas better than the SH sessions stuff but at the end of it just was not clicking like they had grown used to.

In the Highways sessions they got a song done in about a week. In these new sessions it was taking a month or sometimes longer to get a single track together. Part of the problem again is Pilson not being there. There technically was nothing wromg with Jerry, his playing or the kind of person he was. He was just simply not Jeff Pilson and G and Appice had a bond with Pilson and a vibe or chemistry that Jerry was just not tapping into for whatever reason.

Already at this point those fans that I mentioned in my forward who live in Whoville and have 2.5 kids and won't go out in the dark by themselves were whining about the direction of the previous release. They wanted the plodding of "Holy Diver" or "Heaven and Hell," which is great if it were 1980 or 1983. It is funny how many people have since come over from the dark side and now say wow what a great album "Strange Highways" is and that Tracy is what he is, a great guitar player. These same people for whatever reason were dogging both initially. Maybe they moved out of Whoville, I don't know, but I can assure you their heart is still there.

These people cried about the old stuff live too. " Oh the solos are not the same as before; he is killing the songs" they would say. Well, why don't we all go put on black pants, white shirts with a red and blue stripe in it and a jacket with a little insignia on it. Then we can all dye our hair the same color put on black framed nerd glasses and be known as number 1 or 2 or 169 or whatever it may be. Believe it or not, but these people were actually catching Ronnie's ear.

The great thing about Tracy though was that he did not play the same old licks over and over that every guitar player that came before him abused. He was unique in his style so if there is not going to be solos or shortened solos then we have some cool overtones for ya to take up that slack.

So time went on through the summer and into the fall trying to work on this new material. By the time they got to November it was becoming increasingly frustrating for everyone. G and Vinny both just could not believe some of the ideas that were getting canned that they could not finish. They had about four songs in all at this point after working since May on the project. It was like there was too much thinking going on in the process. Songs were being pieced together with many different parts to them so unlike Highways. It just was not the natural creative ebb and flow and it was affecting everyone during the project.

A well-deserved and needed break from the writing was finally here. The band had a series of dates to play in South America and they all needed it.

27.11.1995	Palace	Sao Paulo/SP		Brazil
28.11.1995	Palace	Sao Paulo/SP		Brazil
29.11.1995	Palace	Sao Paulo/SP		Brazil
30.11.1995	Chocolate Chic	Curitiba/PR		Brazil
02.12.1995	New Time	Florianopolis/SC	Zawajus	Brazil

This was Tracy's first ever trip to South America. He could not believe the fans reaction to the band. Not only did they come to the shows in the thousands but they also chased their bus screaming and crying to meet the band, They would mob restaurants where they were eating and just treating them like they were gods. It was a very uplifting experience for Tracy and a great break to help the guys forget the experience that was going on in the writing process.

Once back home from that 2 week run of dates it was back to things ever changing. Gone from the band now was Jerry Best. Ronnie just did not feel it was working with him so he was being replaced. Back in the band now was Jeff Pilson. Tracy, as well as all the guys, were excited to have their partner in crime back with them and all breathed a sigh of relief.

The excitement of Jeff's re entry into the band was a very short lived one. Even though the "Strange Highways" lineup was back in place it was still not right. True there was some energy back and it felt great but Jeff for one was not in full board like before. At this time he had Dokken back and firing away and it was no secret that the Dokken camp was not thrilled about him being in Dio at the same time.

The next odd happening and even clearer sign that something was not right was a song selection. At the very start of Jeff's being back in the band Ronnie announced that they would be doing a song that Jeff had brought with him into rehearsals. Tracy thought OK to some degree but when he found out that it was basically going to be like doing a cover tune he was floored. Not only were they learning the music as it was on the demo but Ronnie was going to use the melody and the lyrics as they were. Now it is not known but not likely that this ever happened before in the past on any Dio release ever. It is documented however that a very similar situation happened on the Black Sabbath "Dehumanizer" release with the song "Master of Insanity." This song was originally written and demo'd in 1991 by Geezer Butler's band in 1991 with Carl Sentence on vocals. After the announcement of "Stay Out Of My Mind" was going to be used Ronnie then said at least we are one song closer to being done with this thing referring to the project as a whole.

There are two things that come to mind when problems like this come up. People either want to say it is the new guy's fault, which in this case is Tracy G, or that there is a problem inside the band or with the one calling the shots. Ronnie had been doing this for decades and he has had his classic releases and he has had his not-so-classic releases as well through decades of recording. It is never easy following a release that just brought the world to its knees like "Strange Highways," "Holy Diver," "Heaven and Hell" or "Dehumanizer." There has never been a DIO release that was clearly a complete failure but there had been some prior to G being in the band that were not DIO to the core or up to those expectations. "Dream Evil" and "Lock Up the Wolves" were both releases like that, but they had some great stuff on them as well.

It is not uncommon for bands to have writer's block or feel pressure from things outside. Not only was Dio following a groundbreaking release but they were also in the middle of the weakest presence of hard rock and metal in the world since the mid '70's during the Disco era. This time Grunge was the musical monster growing overnight to gargantuan size, birthing a huge onslaught of new music that flooded into the marketplace taking a ferocious bite out of the genre Dio lived in. All of that pressure had to have some effect on the band whether they realized it or not at the time while going through this release's writing process. It is hard for fans who do not have a background in being a musician to understand writer's block and what that vice-like pressure can do to you while trying to create. At the end of the day it takes the band as a whole to put all of this together and what effects one person or two has an impact on the group.

True that some of the longtime hard-core fans of Dio were not sure of what to make of the new Dio and the approach of

"Strange Highways" but many also loved what they were hearing. Even on "SH" if things were in that pretty little box of 4/4 timing (which is the norm in most music) the band found a way to give it a new feel and make it fresh. It was music at its best and even Ronnie has gone on record as saying that SH was a refreshing approach and would probably go down as the most underappreciated Dio release. He then went on to say in years to come when people go back and listen to it they would realize how great of an album it was and how it was the "Mob Rules" of the Dio releases. That seems to be coming true.

The simple fact that the previous sessions took about a total of 13 weeks to get ready and this one took just at a year in all speaks volumes. There was riff after riff, jam after jam and day after day coming and going with nothing being accomplished. It was a complete one 180-degree turn from the Highway's release. That release to this day stands up against anything that comes out today and sounds phenomenal with unreal songs.

There were so many great ideas just thrown away that it had built up some frustration with Tracy and Vinny. They had some great stuff there and knew it so they were starting to look for a side project to get these ideas to fruition. They were not leaving Dio or anything of that type. They also did not want to cause any friction in the Dio camp but needed an outlet for what they had. In Tracy's spare time he put together a demo of songs at the "G" Factory studio's for them to look for a vocalist. Vinny then took the demo and went out and got two of the most unlikely people you would think for this heavy demo's. In walked with much enthusiasm Phil Mogg and Pete Way from UFO.

The two UFO members flew over to California for a couple days and rehearsed the tunes and then the four piece went into the studio and cut two tracks. These tracks did get a deal for them in Japan but do to busy schedules with UFO and DIO the four were never able to take advantage of what they had created. I for one would have loved to of heard an entire release from that session.

Back to the angry confused machines now. With the sessions finally finished it was time to enter the studio. As mentioned at the top of this chapter this was too changed from the previous project. Jeff Pilson had introduced Ronnie to Wyn Davis at Total Access studio in Redondo Beach, California. This was a much smaller studio than before so even the way they tracked was not exactly the ideal way as Vinny, Tracy and Jeff were all in the drum tracking room and Ronnie was in another room.

Jeff was also not present as much as the Highway's project, basically only being there for his parts. He was also absent from the photo shoot of this project as again the Dokken camp was applying some pressure so Dio for the first time ever shot the promo shots as a trio with Dio, Appice and G.

For Tracy the studio was much different from the first trip in. This time Ronnie was wanting certain things that were totally against his way of playing and there again was the pressure that was felt during the writing process. It is not to say that anyone was wrong or that the band dis liked one another. That was not even the case at all. This was one of those times that you experience as a musician and creator especially if you have been in it for any time. True Tracy was only on Dio project number two but he had been writing and recording for years.

It is also important to understand that the band was playing great. Vinny, Jeff and G were all on top of their games as players and Ronnie's voice sounded as amazing as ever. There are some great highlights to the Angry release as well. From my own point of view I think this release could have been on the level of "Strange Highways" if only the same approach for the production had been taken. The sounds of the two releases are night and day. The bigger sound of Highways absolutely is what a band of Dio's style should always have and I think the sound of Angry was too thin with not enough depth. Of course my version I listen to does now as I fixed that but it is still not the same as Highways.

Once the album was completed another new step was made as well. "Strange Highways" had been mastered by George Marino at Sterling Sound, New York City. Angry was mastered by Eddy Schreyer at Oasis Mastering in Los Angeles. Just another step of difference in the entire process.

Every step that was taken (again my perception only) was clearly a down grade from the "Strange Highways" process except for Wyn Davis. Wyn is a highly accomplished engineer and producer but really had little to do except for engineering in this process. When everything is taken into account it is easy to see a world of difference in the process from the predecessor.

Now with it all done the next step is to get into rehearsals and hit the road and this release was going to see a long road in front of it but where better to experience DIO than in a concert setting.

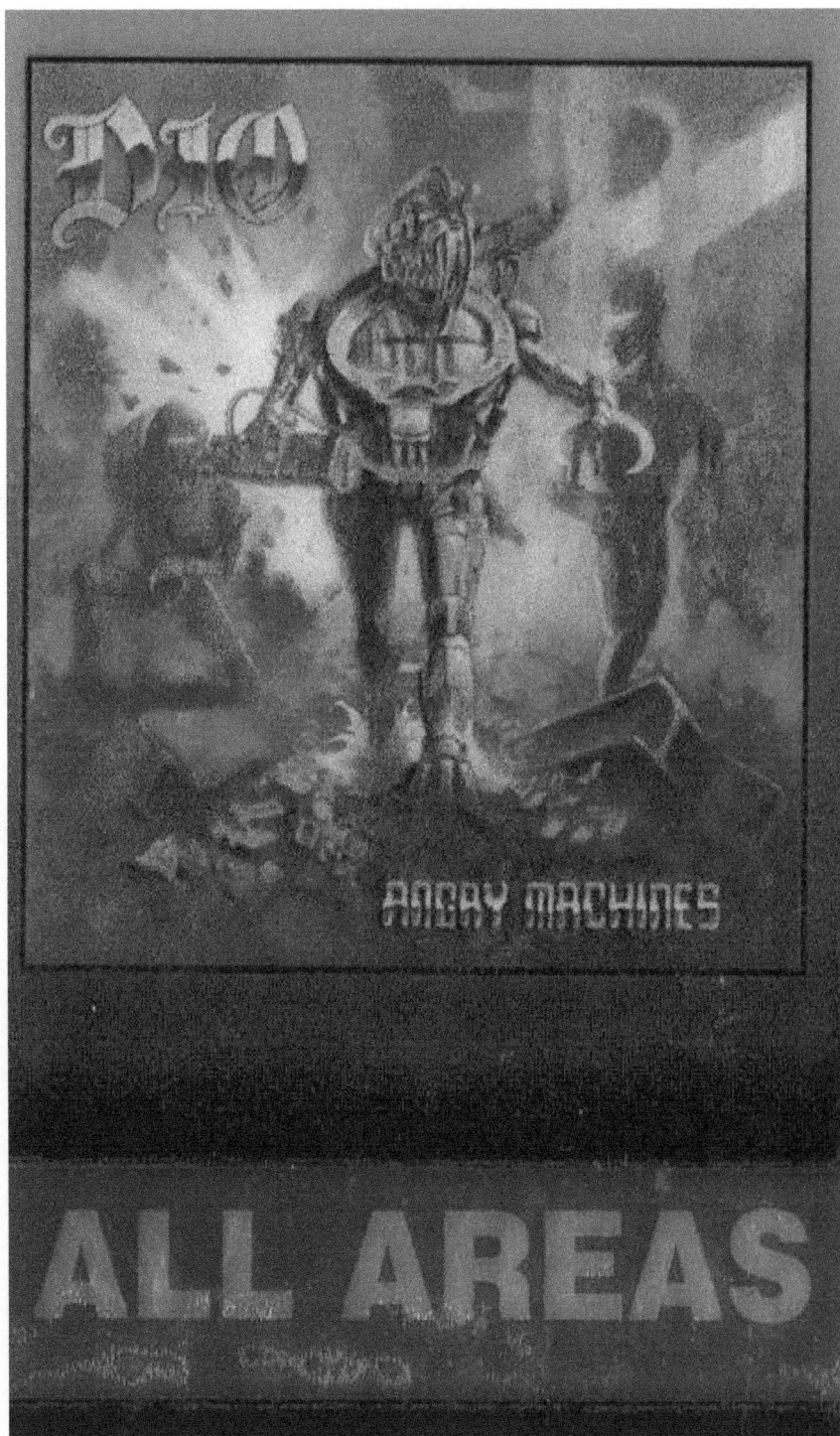

THE MANY MILES TOUR

So with the CD done and the release just a few weeks away it was time to find a touring bass player. There was not much time to spare in this either as the tour was already scheduled and set to start just three weeks after the CD's release. It seems that ever since Tracy G landed the gig in DIO, the band had an ever-growing problem with bass players. First Bain, then Pilson and onto Best and back to Pilson and now yet another name.

So the first thing to do was to find that guy. Being in a band with the name DIO meant that there was never a shortage of people wanting to have their crack at being in the band. Tryouts were very limited and it came down to two different players. One guy who reminded the band of Flea from the Chili Peppers a bit because of his style and look and the other guy being from the school of rock look. Also number two had played on two Tony MacAlpine releases which also made him more of a fit for the DIO sound.

The lucky winner was Larry Dennison. As Tracy had put it, "There was a discussion between me and Ronnie about both players and while they both could really play well Larry just had the "it factor" for the DIO band and time served with MaCalpine helped to so he got the gig."

So with little time to spare the band rearranged the rehearsal space from the writing sessions of "Angry Machines" into the preproduction space for a tour. This tour was going to be quite more involved than the previous one as well. The "Angry Machines" tour would see 129 shows in all and the

"Strange Highways" would see around 100 shows in support. The difference was that the AM tour would see Europe twice, Japan, the United States, Canada and the final stop was in South America. The "Strange Highways" tour only saw one early stint in Europe and the rest was in the United States. Then there was that little South America oh-by-the-way run that happened during the writing session for "Angry Machines."

So while the dates were not all that many more, the miles were and that will wipe you out in a hurry. The excitement of the travel however counters that so the energy and adrenaline level is always cranked on high.

With a bass player found it was time to get to work. The first day of the "Angry Machines" tour rehearsal was here and Tracy shows up to the facility ready to work and do the thing he loves most and that is getting ready to play live. As much as any musician loves to create; the charge you get from playing live far exceeds the studio rush.

The other thing that you get excited about is the set list as well. As with most DIO tours this was to change as well in an attempt to keep the show fresh for the fans. When you have a back log of material in abundance like Ronnie does there is always so many cool things to pull from and have that surprise in there as well that it makes it fun for the fans to experience with the band.

The rehearsals went really well with Larry. He was up to speed very quickly and was a fast study which was nice to have a tight band going into a year long string of dates. It was still not Jeff Pilson but Larry was not far from him and made the situation very comfortable.

The set list for this tour also was much different from the previous tour as well as we just noted. Only JMHG made it into the set this tour and then only two new ones from the new release made it as well but they were never the same all the time. Bouncing around from a selection of four from that release but it was mostly "Hunter of the Heart" and "Double Monday." The majority of the tour's set list was as follows

* Intro

* "Jesus, Mary and the Holy Ghost"

* "Straight into the Heart"

* "Don't Talk to Strangers"

* "Holy Diver"

* - drum solo

* "Heaven and Hell"

* "Double Monday"

* "Stand up and Shout"

* "Hunter of the Heart"

* "Mistreated"

* "Catch the Rainbow"

* Guitar solo

* "Mistreated" (reprise) (some nights throwing in "Man on the Silver Mountain" and "Long Live Rock n Roll")

* "Last in Line"

* Encore: "Rainbow in the Dark," and "Mob Rules"

The way that "Mistreated" got into the set was totally by accident. Tracy recalled one day at rehearsals he was noodling around and was playing the signature riff from "Mistreated." He remembered that Ronnie whipped around and looked at him and said how he loved that song. Tracy was blown away and quickly said to him, "Let's do it then." Of course being from Blackmore made it great with Tracy as well. So from that point on it was a nightly part of the show.

The first night of the tour was a much different set list and a shame it did not continue through the entire tour but with that said here is how the tour's set started out.

* "Jesus, Mary and the Holy Ghost"

* "Straight Through the Heart"

* "After All (The Dead)"

* "Evilution"

* "Big Sister"

* "Stand Up and Shout"

* "Hunter of the Heart"

* "Heaven and Hell"

* "I"

* "Double Monday"

* "Mistreated"

* "Rainbow in the Dark"

* "Last in Line"

* "Don't Talk to Strangers"

* "Institutional Man"

* "The Mob Rules"

This is a set list that was intended for both the traditional fan and the new fan that the G era was attracting. There was a combination of five of the new era songs and on top of that there were songs in the set from the most recent Sabbath release as well. If this attitude would have continued, in this writer's own opinion, DIO could of grown to new heights never seen. Also in this set from time to time there would be an inclusion of "Big Sister" from the AM release.

The tour opened up in sunny California at the Ventura Theater in the city of Ventura. All the dates were going great with different opening bands for just about every stop until about the tenth show in. In Houston, Texas, they picked up Motorhead and were with them for the next 26 shows that went all the way through the first run of European dates that were in Germany and Austria. Ronnie and Lemmy were old friends and the two liked to tour together so this was a good fit and made for a great one-two punch for the fans.

07.11.1996	Ventura Theater	Ventura, CA	USA
08.11.1996	Municipal Auditorium	Riverside, CA	USA
09.11.1996	Galaxy Theatre	Santa Ana, CA	USA
10.11.1996	Rockin' Rodeo	Bakersfield, CA	USA
12.11.1996	The Beach	Las Vegas, NV	USA
13.11.1996	Electric Ballroom	Tempe, AZ	USA
14.11.1996	Midnight Rodeo	Albuquerque, NM	USA
15.11.1996	19th Street Warehouse	Lubbock, TX	USA

17.11.1996	West Park Entertainment Center	Houston, TX	USA
18.11.1996	Sneaker's	San Antonio, TX	USA
19.11.1996	Yellow Rose	Corpus Christi, TX	USA
20.11.1996	Villa Real	McAllen, TX	USA
22.11.1996	Cain's Ballroom	Tulsa, OK	USA
23.11.1996	Toy Tiger	Louisville, KY	USA
24.11.1996	Alrosa Villa	Columbus, OH	USA
25.11.1996	Annie's	Cincinnati, OH	USA
27.11.1996	The Strand	Providence, RI	USA
28.11.1996	Birch Hill	Old Bridge, NJ	USA
30.11.1996	The Roxy	New York, NY	USA
02.12.1996	E.M. Loews Palladium	Worcester, MA	USA
03.12.1996	Toad's Place	New Haven, CT	USA
04.12.1996	Jaxx	Springfield, VA	USA
08.12.1996	Freiheitshalle	Hof	Germany
09.12.1996	Filharmonia	Filderstadt	Germany
11.12.1996	C23	Munich	Germany
12.12.1996	Sporthalle	Augsburg	Germany
13.12.1996	Eberthalle	Ludwigshafen	Germany
15.12.1996	Libro(music)hall	Vienna	Austria
16.12.1996	Stadthalle	Furth	Germany

17.12.1996	Arena	Berlin	Germany
18.12.1996	Haus Auensee	Leipzig	Germany
20.12.1996	Christmas Circus (Tent)	Gottingen	Germany
21.12.1996	Music Hall	Hannover	Germany
22.12.1996	Gaswerk	Hamburg	Germany
23.12.1996	Biskuithalle	Bonn	Germany

During that run of dates everyone got sick. Ronnie had went on record as saying that the bus they had was very drafty and Germany and Austria in the middle of December no matter what year it is always going to be extremely cold. So as the string of dates went on the entire crew and band got colds and Vinny Appice ended up with pneumonia out of it.

Even after a month Vinny was still too sick to get back behind the kit. The band was scheduled to go back out in support of the new release on February 6, 1997. Waiting until the last minute to see if Vinny was going to be able to do it left them little to no time to get someone to fill in. It is tough to get someone at the last minute to not only fill in but to also learn the show so that it flows well for the fans' experience.

So with little time Ronnie called his good friends in the Scorpions camp and asked for a loaner on James Kottak for five or six dates or until Vinny could come back. Ronnie's relationship with the Scorpions has always been a very close one and James got right on board and off they went. James went on to play San Juan Capistrano, West Hollywood, San Diego, Palo Alto and San Francisco California with Vinny returning to his stool in Seattle, Washington on Feb. 13, 1997.

06.02.1997 Coach House San Juan Capistrano, CA   USA

07.02.1997	Billboard Live	West Hollywood, CA	USA
08.02.1997	Brick By Brick	San Diego, CA	USA
10.02.1997	The Edge	Palo Alto, CA	USA
11.02.1997	Trocadero	San Francisco, CA	USA
13.02.1997	Ballard Firehouse	Seattle, WA	USA
14.02.1997	Ballard Firehouse	Seattle, WA	USA
15.02.1997	Roseland Theater	Portland, OR	USA
16.02.1997	Crest Theater	Sacramento, CA	USA

Those types of situations are always stressful because of the unknown factor of what the new guy does and does not know and Tracy was the unsaid band leader in those situations for cue's etc with the new drummer. The styles of James and Vinny were and are very similar so the playing itself is not so odd just the little cues that Tracy and the other guys had become accustomed to over the years playing with Vinny.

So Vinny got back just in time to go back to Europe right in the dead of winter and where else to go except to Viking country where it was sure to be colder than hell especially for a California boy like Tracy who had never in his life seen or witnessed what was about to hit him.

That tour had 23 dates (many first time stops for G) in Europe starting Feb 20 in Estonia, Finland, Sweden, Norway and then back into Germany and then eventually south to Spain where it was a bit warmer only to go back north again.

20.02.1997	Club Dekoltee	Tallinn	Estonia
21.02.1997	Tavastia Club	Helsinki	Finland
23.02.1997	Electric Garden	Stockholm	Sweden
24.02.1997	Rockefeller	Oslo	Norway
25.02.1997	Metron	Gothenburg	Sweden
26.02.1997	Vega	Copenhagen	Denmark
27.02.1997	Multihus Tobaksfarikk	Esbjerg	Denmark
02.03.1997	The Aladin	Bremen	Germany
03.03.1997	Paradiso	Amsterdam	Netherlands
04.03.1997	Vooruit	Gent	Belgium
05.03.1997	Elysee Montmartre	Paris	France
07.03.1997	Canciller	Madrid	Spain
08.03.1997	Sala Gares	Pamplona	Spain
09.03.1997	Zeleste	Barcelona	Spain
10.03.1997	Transclub	Lyon	France
13.03.1997	Konzertfabrik 27	Pratteln	Switzerland
14.03.1997	Atomic Love	Pordenone	Italy
16.03.1997	Festhalle	Tuttlingen	Germany
17.03.1997	Musichalle Q	Regensburg	Germany
18.03.1997	Palac Akropolis	Prague	Czech Republic

19.03.1997 Lokomotiva Sport Hall   Pilsen   Czech Republic

20.03.1997 Petofi Csarnok   Budapest   Hungary

23.03.1997 Astoria   London   UK

At one point the band was to go across the Gulf of Bothnia between Finland and Sweden only to find it frozen. Tracy could not believe what he was seeing not too mention he really did not bring the right gear to wear for this type of cold weather. It was a totally different experience than he had ever been through before. Tracy G loved the people and the gigs but the weather and the difference in the styles of food from back home and in Europe just really messed with him a bit. Little problems in the scheme of things but in no way a deal breaker so to speak.

This tour marked a lot of firsts for Tracy. Seeing that kind of cold weather and the majority of Europe for the first time to include the Czech Republic, Hungary and the Nordic region just to mention a few.

March 23, 1997, ended the European run of the "Angry Machines" tour in London at the Astoria to a sold-out crowd of 2,000 people. Dio in the European theater had never lost its draw or its power. Always playing to big crowds for the most part and a few smaller venues as they had always done. In the States, however, the music scene was in chaos with fads ever-changing, and that has stayed in effect to the present day. You can play to a crowd of 2,000 or 5,000 one night and 500 the next.

So with a week off the band resumed another run of 24 dates in the United States and then after that it was off to Japan for the first time since August of 1986. This again was another first for Tracy and a very cool one at that.

02.04.1997	Outback	Tuscon, AZ	USA
04.04.1997	Tonie's	Colorado Springs, CO	USA
05.04.1997	Ogden Theatre	Denver, CO	USA
06.04.1997	Cowboys	Wichita, KS	USA
08.04.1997	Pop's Annex	Sauget, IL	USA
09.04.1997	Medusa's	Kansas City, MO	USA
11.04.1997	Jackhammer's	Schaumburg, IL	USA
12.04.1997	Body Shop	Goshin, IN	USA
13.04.1997	Rocker	Grand Rapids, MI	USA
14.04.1997	Vogue Theatre	Indianapolis, IN	USA
16.04.1997	The Edge	Des Moines, IA	USA
17.04.1997	Rave	Milwaukee, WI	USA
18.04.1997	Medina Entertainment Center	Medina, MN	USA
19.04.1997	The Checkered Flag	Appleton, WI	USA
20.04.1997	State Theatre	Detroit, MI	USA
22.04.1997	Warehouse	Toronto, ON	Canada
24.04.1997	Machine	Massillon, OH	USA
25.04.1997	Rainbow Gardens	Erie, PA	USA
26.04.1997	Ogden St. Concert Hall	Buffalo, NY	USA
27.04.1997	X-Hale	Frederick, MD	USA
29.04.1997	Village Nightclub	Lancaster, PA	USA

30.04.1997	A1A	Lexington, KY	USA
01.05.1997	Silo	Reading, PA	USA
02.05.1997	Chance	Poughkeepsie, NY	USA
07.05.1997	Umeda Heat Beat	Osaka	Japan
08.05.1997	Bottom Line	Nagoya	Japan
10.05.1997	Club Citta	Kawasaki	Japan
11.05.1997	Club Citta	Kawasaki	Japan
20.05.1997	Egan Center	Anchorage, AK	USA
21.05.1997	Studebakers	Burnaby, BC	Canada
22.05.1997	Cowboy's Concert Hall	Calgary, AB	Canada
23.05.1997	Thunderdome	Edmunton, BC	Canada
25.05.1997	Ballard Firehouse	Seattle, WA	USA
27.05.1997	The Grizzly Rose	Golden, CO	USA
28.05.1997	Ranch Bowl	Omaha, NE	USA
29.05.1997	Big Dogs	Cedar Rapids, IA	USA
30.05.1997	Sand Bar	Arena, WI	USA
31.05.1997	Vic Theater	Chicago, IL	USA
02.06.1997	Mabel's	Champaign, IL	USA

03.06.1997	Caliber Club	Bay City, MI	USA
04.06.1997	Papa Joe's	Dayton, OH	USA
05.06.1997	Sycamore Gardens	Cincinnati, OH	USA
07.06.1997	Agora Theater	Cleveland, OH	USA
08.06.1997	Sault Outdoor Festival	Eckerman, MI	USA
09.06.1997	The Embassy Concert Club	London, ON	Canada
10.06.1997	Water Street Music Hall	Rochester, NY	USA
12.06.1997	Hampton Beach Casino		
13.06.1997	CPI	Hampton Bays, NY	USA
14.06.1997	Webster Theater	Hartford, CT	USA
15.06.1997	TLA	Philadelphia, PA	USA
17.06.1997	Tink's	Scranton, PA	USA
18.06.1997	Strand	Providence, RI	USA
20.06.1997	Budweiser Summer Sound Stage	Big Flats, NY	USA
21.06.1997	Birch Hill NC	Old Bridge, NJ	USA
22.06.1997	Tuxedo Junction	Danbury, CT	USA
23.06.1997	7 Willow Street	Port Chester, NY	USA
15.11.1997	Skol Festival, Estadio do Caninde	Sao Paulo	Brazil
16.11.1997	Mineirinho	Belo Horizonte	Bra

18.11.1997	Metropolitan	Rio De Janeiro	Brazil
19.11.1997	Marumbi Expo Center	Curitiba	Brazil
21.11.1997	Estadio Santa Laura	Santiago	Chile
23.11.1997	Estadio Obras Sanitarias	Buenos Aires	Argentina

The overseas stuff was a great experience, except that this time around unlike the previous tour Tracy was using rental gear in the foreign countries. With the tour so extensive and so much they opted to use a punch list for gear with the promoters over carrying their own not only for the convenience factor but the cost as well. Going from country to country in Europe and a lot of flying really increased the chances of lost gear, broken gear and the cost was astronomical as well. It is tough using unknown gear for a player and especially when you have your own sound and you know that nothing you get even if it is exact will still sound like your stuff that has been tweaked over time just for you. What do you do you ask? You learn to adjust and go with it and Tracy did as did the entire band.

So on Nov. 23, 1997 the "Angry Machines" world tour officially came to an end. A ton of miles, a ton of people and a ton of hours spent making people smile all over the world. And for Tracy many new places such as Japan and Finland for Tracy to play and make new friends and fans.

Now time to decompress and get ready for the next DIO move.

TO HULL AND WHAT

So as always it was a few months off before the next adventure. This time instead of getting together and writing a new opus there would be a live album to support.

During the "Angry Machines" tour there were several shows that were recorded live for a live release. In interviews it was said that Chicago was the place where the live recording originated from. In the liner notes however for the Japan release of the "Live Inferno" release there are multiple places that the recording were supposed to have came from.

The two bonus tracks of the Black Sabbath songs "After All" and "I" from the Dehumanizer release of 1992 were included on the Japan release and were recorded in Riverside, California at the start of the tour.

There is always the debate too about how much of a live release is actually live and how much is not? In case you have not heard and you are big KISS fan none of Alive or Alive two is live except the drums. "The Live Evil" Black Sabbath release is only Appice and Dio live with Iommi and Butler replaying their parts.

This is not that there are not true live releases out there. According to everyone the Rainbow "Live on Stage" release is totally live. The live at Radio City Music Hall release from "Heaven and Hell" is supposed to be all live as well but have you ever noticed what seems to sound like rhythm guitar way down in the mix during certain solo sections? I know it may come as a big shock to many of you and not such a shock to others but it all a fact.

About the only thing that you just can not fix in these situations are the drums. This is even more so when dealing with Vinny Appice. Vinny drops many sticks during a show and it has always been that way. Not only does he just beat the hell out of the kit but he holds the stick in his right hand which is his hi-hat and ride cymbal hand between his index and middle fingers and that cause a lot of drops throughout the show.

That is not the only reason but just take my word for it that trying to do a fix as it is called on a drum set is just not doable for the live release. You have not only the drum mics but also the room mics, P.A. mics and the other instrument mics that are all picking up the drums as the recording and playing are going on and the slightest change - if it is the slightest bit off - will screw everything up and make it very obvious.

Talking about all of this must lead to something right? Well, it does so as it relates to the "Live Inferno" release as well. On this release there were fixes made for the final product by both Tracy and Larry Dennison at Ronnie and Wyn Davis request. Angry Machines was just the start of a long relationship between Ronnie and Wyn that would last until Ronnie's passing in 2010.

So Tracy went in and did his fixes to help the things that needed done. It was not a total replay of the album mind you but just a few little things that resulted from a broken string or something of that nature. Same for the bass; very minor and quick.

So after those things were taken care of it was time to mix the album. Good thing about a live mix is that you go in and clean up anything that may need it and be sure that everything is in line and then it just runs. You do a little bit of fader movements in the songs for solos etc., but they are for the most part very easy to mix. As a mix engineer in the studio it is one of those cases that the pay seems worth it because of the time put into it.

Now for the live effort of this release it was both necessary and obvious that the drum solo and guitar solo were cut down for the products release. Both Vinny and Tracy had much longer solos in the actual live show but for the releases sake and the fact that only so much music will fit on a CD they had to be edited.

This is the one and only day that Tracy was not at the studio for the mix down. Of course, it would be during that day they edit his guitar solo right? It actually was not that big of a deal since it was not in its entirety and you were going to lose the full effect of it anyhow.

Now as far as what city did song so and so come from on the release the only two people who really know that is Dio himself and Wyn Davis. It really in the end does not matter as it all sounds really good but still I know I would like to know.

I, for one, would of loved to have seen the early set list from the "Angry Machines" tour to have been the one that was used for this live product. Of course, I expect certain things to always be in a DIO show but I also want to have representation of the newest things as well. To add the most recent Sabbath material along with more cuts off of Highways and Machines would have made for a more compelling and interesting product not only for me but a lot of other fans out there as well.

During the mixing of this product though one day when Tracy G arrived for mixing Ronnie and Davis asked him his thoughts on the over all sound? G responded by telling them that it sounded to him too much like a studio record and that it needed more room and ambiance to the overall sound. They both listened back and agreed with him and made the change to it.

Upon listening to my CD of the Japan release I still think it could have used a bit more. I would have liked to have had more of the room and P.A. mics for the overall sound but the reason for it not being in the mix more may be to a fix here and there and not being able to mix it in that fashion. The only way to know that would be to talk to Wyn Davis and we did not have the time to get him on the interview process.

The live release took right around two to three weeks to finish up totally. This included the mix and mastering. The live CD was to get its release on Feb. 24, 1998. Unlike the previous releases with Tracy, this tour did not start right on the heels of the release.

The official " To Hull and Back" tour was not to start for another three months so it left some more down time for the band to relax and enjoy family and friends. This tour was going to be another nice little trip that would include 80 some dates in all and would include the first ever trip into Russia for the DIO band.

19.05.1998	Rockin' Rodeo	Bakersfield, CA	USA
20.05.1998	Crossroads	Yucaipa, CA	USA
22.05.1998	Maritime Hall	San Francisco, CA	USA
23.05.1998	The Joint	Las Vegas, NV	USA

24.05.1998	Cajun House	Scottsdale, AZ	USA
25.05.1998	'Canes	San Diego, CA	USA
28.05.1998	Midnight Rodeo	Albuquerque, NM	USA
29.05.1998	Ogden Theater	Denver, CO	USA
31.05.1998	In Cahoots	Oklahoma City, OK	USA
01.06.1998	Roadhouse Ruby's	Kansas City, MO	USA
02.06.1998	In Cahoots	Wichita, KS	USA
03.06.1998	Pop's Annex	Sauget, IL	USA
05.06.1998	M.E.C.	Medina, MN	USA
06.06.1998	Rave Bar	Milwaukee, WI	USA
08.06.1998	Soft Tail Lounge	Rantoul, IL	USA
09.06.1998	Nik's Ivanhoe	Pekin, IL	USA
11.06.1998	Piere's Night Club	Fort Wayne, IN	USA
12.06.1998	Annie's	Cincinnati, OH	USA
13.06.1998	Toy Tiger	Louisville, KY	USA
15.06.1998	Jaxx	Springfield, VA	USA
16.06.1998	Daytona's	Riviera Beach, MD	USA
18.06.1998	The Fun House	Buffalo, NY	USA
19.06.1998	Birch Hill Night Club	Old Bridge, NJ	USA
20.06.1998	The Chance	Poughkeepsie, NY	USA
22.06.1998	House Of Blues	Myrtle Beach, SC	USA

23.06.1998	Grady Cole Center	Charlotte, NC	USA
24.06.1998	Outer Edge	Marietta, GA	USA
26.06.1998	Riviera Theatre	Chicago, IL	USA
27.06.1998	B.D. Pavillion	Columbus, OH	USA
28.06.1998	Copps Coliseum	Hamilton, ON	Canada
30.06.1998	Wings Stadium	Kalamazoo, MI	USA
01.07.1998	Pine Knob Music	Clarkston, MI	USA
02.07.1998	Nautica Stage	Cleveland, OH	USA
04.07.1998	Stade du' Murier	Montreal, PQ	Canada
05.07.1998	L'Agora	Quebec City, PQ	Canad
07.07.1998	Roseland Ballroom	New York City, NY	USA
10.07.1998	Sunken Garden Amphitheatre	San Antonio, TX	USA
11.07.1998	The Road House	San Benito, TX	US
12.07.1998	Coca-Cola Starplex Amphitheatre	Dallas, TX	US
14.07.1998	Celebrity Theater	Phoenix, AZ	USA
02.08.1998	Universal Amphitheater	Universal City, CA	USA
03.08.1998	SDSU Open Air Theater	San Diego, CA	USA
20.09.1998	Festivalna Hall	Sofia	Bulgaria

21.09.1998	Polyvalent Hall	Bucharest	Romani
23.09.1998	Nachtverk	Munich	Germany
24.09.1998	Alte Feuerwache	Mannheim	Germany
25.09.1998	Ludwigshalle	Dieburg	Germany
26.09.1998	Capitol	Hannover	Germany
27.09.1998	Forum	Nurnberg	Germany
29.09.1998	Docks	Hamburg	Germany
30.09.1998	Columbiahalle	Berlin	Germany
02.10.1998	Kalle Werk Bad	Salzungen	Germany
03.10.1998	Schutzenhaus	Markneukirchen	Germany
04.10.1998	Rockfabrik	Ludwigsburg	Germany
05.10.1998	Take Off	Ulm	Germany
07.10.1998	FBZ	Braunschweig	Germany
08.10.1998	Biscuithalle	Bonn	Germany
09.10.1998	Kulturhalle	Merchweiler	Germany
10.10.1998	Z7	Pratteln	Switzerland
12.10.1998	Transclub	Lyon	France
13.10.1998	Zeleste	Barcelona	Spain
15.10.1998	Macumba	Madrid	Spain
16.10.1998	Sala Quattro	Aviles	Spain
17.10.1998	Gares	Pamplona	Spain

19.10.1998	Elysee Montmartre	Paris	France
20.10.1998	Noorderligt	Tilburg	Netherlands
22.10.1998	Forum	London	UK
23.10.1998	K2 Fregatten	Akersberga	Sweden
24.10.1998	Garvarn	Ljungby	Sweden
26.10.1998	Pumpehuset	Copenhage	Denmark
28.10.1998	Kulturbolaget (KB)	Malmo	Sweden
29.10.1998	Folkets Park/Hus	Gavle	Sweden
30.10.1998	Jager	Karlstad	Sweden
31.10.1998	Lisbergshallen	Gothenburg	Sweden
01.11.1998	Rockefeller	Oslo	Norway
03.11.1998	Tavastia	Helsinki	Finland
05.11.1998	Saga	Ostersund	Sweden
06.11.1998	Skonsbergs Folkets Hus	Sundsvall	Sweden
07.11.1998	Kulturhuset Jonkoping	Jonkoping	Sweden
04.03.1999	Yubileiny Sports Palace	St. Petersburg	Russia
05.03.1999	Olimpiyskey Stadium	Moscow	Russia

So as usual it was time to get to the rehearsal hall and get ready to get the tour together. From day one again this was going to be a pain in the ass for everyone.

When Tracy arrived to start the process of practice he was right from the get-go slapped in the face with a huge hole in the middle of the room where Vinny's drums were supposed to be. Ronnie looked at Tracy and said "we have no drummer." Tracy was more than a bit confused by this and asked Ronnie what was going on? Black Sabbath had reunited with Ozzy and were embarking on a world tour themselves but Bill Ward was not in good health at all and they wanted Appice to be there in case he was not able to go on. The basic result is that it came down to more money being offered from the Sabbath camp.

Ronnie also told Tracy that he had called Simon Wright to come down and start rehearsals for the tour. Then a call came in from Wendy that Vinny was going to do it and now a new decision had to be made. Do you go with Vinny knowing that if the call comes from Sabbath that he will most likely go or do you go with Simon?

Tracy hated the thought of not playing with Vinny but also understood the problems of what might happen if Vinny were to leave in mid stream on the tour and what problems it could cause. Even as much as he hated it he told Ronnie he would go with Simon to avoid the problem but on the other hand Vinny is DIO and he is the one that supplied that DIO swing and helped to create the sound.

After some thought Ronnie agreed with Tracy that Vinny is the DIO sound and so he made the decision to go with Vinny knowing what might happen. That also led to having to call Simon who was on his way to set up and jump in and tell him that he was not needed which also sucked to do that to someone.

So with the early drama gone the band settled into the steps of getting ready for the tour. Once the rehearsals were done and the show was ready it was off to Bakersfield, California for night one of the tour.

Once they arrived they all indeed found out that Vinny was not going to be there for the tour. It was a chance they took and it was one that came back to bite them. This is something that was wrong on a lot of levels. Vinny had made a decision to stay in DIO and do the tour so in my opinion he should have stayed and full filled his obligations. Then there is the fact that Ronnie had kept Vinny in an income for ninety-five percent of his career since his entering Black Sabbath in 1980. Only two years since 1980 had Appice not played in a band with DIO and during that time he was with Tracy.

One would think there would be more loyalty to someone or something especially when they had made a commitment to do something but not in this case.So with the announcement made Ronnie then called Simon Wright back up and told him to pack the drums and get to Bakersfield and start learning things.

Simon had done a previous stint with Ronnie for the "Lock up the Wolves" release and tour in 1990 before Ronnie went back to Sabbath. So he was somewhat familiar with Ronnie's backlog of music which would help out a little. The problem here is that Vinny was leaving after the third show in San Francisco so Simon was really going to have to be on the horse so to speak. Tracy was the guy that put in charge of getting Simon up to speed on things as well. Not only was he going to have to get him up to speed on the songs but they were going to have to get some stage cues down as well for the start and stops of songs. Cues are a thing built over time and normally a natural thing between players so this was going to be very rough to say the least.

Even with the obvious of replacing the position in the band that drives the machine is the fact that the drivers in this position being Appice and Wright are totally different in their style. This move totally made the band one hundred percent different from it had been in 93 and 94. Larry being in the band changed things a bit but not that much. It was still a very happening situation and the band still had that groove and vibe to it even though not totally like when Pilson was there.

The first thing that has to be said is that Simon Wright is a good drummer. He is, actually a perfect drummer for bands like AC/DC and Rhino Bucket and other bands that fit that mold. There is however a certain swing and way that the drums are played in Dio music whether it be Dio or Sabbath or Heaven and Hell. The reason for that is Vinny Appice. This fact can be noticed from The "Mob Rules" release with Sabbath in 81 all the way to "The Devil You Know" with Heaven and Hell in 2009. There is just a certain way the man plays that creates the Dio style and Simon was not the guy to do that.

The Dio sound requires much push and pull and just a feel to it that is unique to Appice. Simon is a very stiff player and very much the 180-degree opposite of the needed style. This does not say that he is not a really good drummer just that his style in what has been created with Appice, Pilson, Dennison and G will be about the same as oil and water. Inside the AC/DC family Simon was brilliant as that music was perfect for his style and it worked brilliantly.

It was at this point that Tracy started to see the writing on the wall so to speak. For the past eight years, minus a few months, Tracy had only played with Appice. He also knew Simon from his days with Angus and Malcolm and knew that it was not going to work the same. He, however, did what a pro would do and rode on for the tour.

Even though the tour carried on and inside a few weeks Simon had settled into things it was still very odd feeling to Tracy. None of the music whether it be the new stuff or the old DIO, Sabbath or Rainbow tunes they were doing felt anywhere near the same. The only way to describe it is to say that it was stiff.

There were many good times on the tour as people, however. As a person and as people the band got along very well. None of that was an issue at all but the feel, the playing and the vibe musically was a big problem for G.

The unsaid law or feeling that is in place when all members of a band or team click together is the most rewarding thing in the world. This unsaid or unwritten thing is that chemistry that makes a band go down as legends or a team that becomes champions or even a dynasty. It is the one little thing that changes that can bring all of that glory to its knees. The one thing that changes can be brilliant as well but when not in sink with what was created or different in its production is all it takes to lose that championship or feel. That is absolutely what happened here.

The one thing that kept even this tough time in a positive was Willie Fyffe. Willie was Ronnie's right hand man and the tour comedian. He always had the right thing to say and was always in a positive frame of mind. For G this was the one thing that was always there other than Ronnie's voice.

So the tour went on to its conclusion which ended in a place the DIO band had never been; Russia. It was then that G was told by someone that they had overheard there were going to be changes in the things for the next product coming up. He had heard about a variety of things but never heard mention of what or who that would be involving but as usual Tracy did not speculate on anything unless he was told personally.

So after the tour was over he was told there would be some time off and then to the next product. He as always had been collecting riffs just for that time.

THE DEPARTURE

So time off was very short in the spring of 1999. Normally there was a couple or three months off from a tour before firing back up or even hearing a sound from anyone. This spring was not to be that way.

In the mail one afternoon Tracy received a package from Ronnie. It was a tape of two songs he had written for the next release which was to be a concept album called "Magica." Now this was odd indeed. Tracy was used to getting in a room with the band and jamming on ideas and riffs until Ronnie picked something out and said OK here it is. In this package was not just an idea but it was a full blown two ideas with Ronnie playing guitar, bass and programming drums as well and, of course, vocals.

The initial reaction to the songs were not great ones from Tracy. They were thought to be very stale and stiff as well. The only thing he could think of was how was he going to spice it up to make it better.

About the same time Wendy had called about a summer European festival tour with the Scorpions that was being booked. She also asked Tracy what he would think about playing rhythm guitar on that tour and them bringing in a classic playing lead guitarist as well? He quickly responded that he didn't think much of it and that he would not be doing that. Wendy went on to ask him to think about it and she would get back to him and he again answered by saying there was no need to think about it that he was not interested.

It was not more than two hours later and Ronnie called Tracy. Tracy asked what was going on and explained the Wendy phone call. Ronnie proceeded to tell him that he was getting it from all sides. The new record company wanted a return to the glory days sound for DIO and that the fans wanted a return to that as well.

Tracy understood what he was saying but he spoke up and said that DIO is a one guitar player band and that he was a one guitar player in a band as well. The new label which was Spitfire Records wanted that old DIO for their product and not the new modern sound that was out there at the time or of the past DIO efforts. Tracy then asked Ronnie what if they got another singer and how would he feel about being asked to share the stage in that way. Ronnie quickly told G that he understood his point and the conversation ended. This was shaping up to being a crazy day and one not to ever be forgotten by G.

An hour after the previous phone call with Ronnie the phone was calling Tracy's name yet again. Again it was Ronnie on the other end. " Let's just forget about that conversation we just had Tracy and move forward." That was just not something G could do fully. He told Dio that it was very strange and privately he felt like the reason for the asking to forget it happened was because they did not have a player in place and needed someone for the tour coming up in the summer. Grijalva went on record by telling his family that he would get a call in about a week releasing him from the band.

It is so funny in the metal world - if that is what you call it. Once you have laid the groundwork for who you are you are not allowed to change it or go in another direction. Bands or artists in this genre also do not attempt to ever stray far from that either. Seems that these bands stereotype themselves or back willingly into a corner and just paint themselves in right there never to leave.

Some bands have tried to expand out from that only to go back like Saxon, Scorpions and now DIO. Bands like Aerosmith however create new things and stick to it and succeed for that. That should be a blue print for people to understand that if you want to go in a different direction and it doesn't work right as you do it to not get wishy-washy on it and to keep going to give it a chance. In this band, for example, they gave it one release being "Strange Highways" and then started to get a little worried that some people did not get it and it affected the next release. Those who get behind decisions and really push it always win at the end of the day which is why Aerosmith a few others can navigate inside the landscape so well and create different factions of fans and make both happy. Stick to your guns.

Well, it did not even take quite a week for that call. Much respect has to be given to the fact that Ronnie did this himself. He called back and told Tracy that he was going to have to let him go. The response was one of understanding and that he had one request of the entire situation and that was to be shown the respect and dignity that was deserved. Ronnie agreed and went on to say that this was not an easy thing to do because he believed in Tracy and what they did together and the fact that he was not an asshole also made it that much harder. Ronnie James Dio had a lot of respect for Tracy Grijalva and it was never a possibility for him to tell G to fuck off or say something bad about him.

This was never more evident than in an interview that was conducted by Alex Richter for Hard n Heavy. Alex Richter: Do you read the music message boards on America Online?

Ronnie James Dio: We have America Online on a laptop and we just came back from Europe and we didn't take the lap top with us. So I haven't even looked at it since I've only been home for a couple of days.

Alex Richter: So in there from time to time, especially today actually, Tracy G has been under fire as being compared to past guitarists you have worked with. Do you have any words for Tracy's critics?

Ronnie James Dio: All I can say is this, they don't play with Tracy. They expect something else from Tracy other than what he is. And Tracy is absolutely a brilliant guitar player. It's a shame more people don't get what Tracy is trying to do. He doesn't want to be the guitar player they expect him to be, they want him to be Richie Blackmore and Tony Iommi and what not. I think he's a combination of all of those people and an individual as well. Tracy G is a real progressive thinker, he plays the kind of music that Vinnie (Appice) and I would want to play and I understand the crap that he takes. I certainly understand that but it's very, very unfair of the criticisms because Tracy is a great guitar player. I love to play with him. He's got a great sense of feel, he's got a great mind, he's a great player. He's just brilliant all the way down the line. People are always going to have critics when they replace people who are really loved by some fans, they are always going to go "oh he doesn't do that, he doesn't do this." But Tracy G is capable of doing absolutely anything. I think he does a better job than anybody I've ever played with. I hate to defend Tracy G, it's terrible to defend somebody who doesn't need any defense, if people don't get it, as far as I'm concerned, they can just fuck off!"

That is a pretty powerful statement coming from not only your boss but an icon that stands above just about all that there ever was. I have often heard Ronnie take defense for something or someone in his camp but never with that coloring to his statements. Tracy was really admired by the man.

At the end of the conversation Tracy told Ronnie that if he ever needed him for any reason that he and his guitar along with Igor would be ready to come to his aide. So the phone call ended peacefully and on a high note of respect from both parties. It came down to being able to fulfill something so that Dio could continue with a label that had some pack to their punch.

Christmas time came that year and Tracy called the DIO management office and left a message to everyone to have a great holiday season. He never got a return call from anyone. He did, however, get a call from Ronnie the following fall right after the Deep Purple tour he was taking part in had concluded. They talked briefly and it was a great conversation and one Tracy remembers but it was also the final ink to the chapter of DIO. That was the final conversation Ronnie and G would ever have together.

Half of G was very sad to see his time in DIO come to an end but the other half was very excited because he did not want to be part of the return to the original DIO sound. He wanted to continue on with what he was about and vowed never to get into that situation again and to this day he has stayed true to his word.

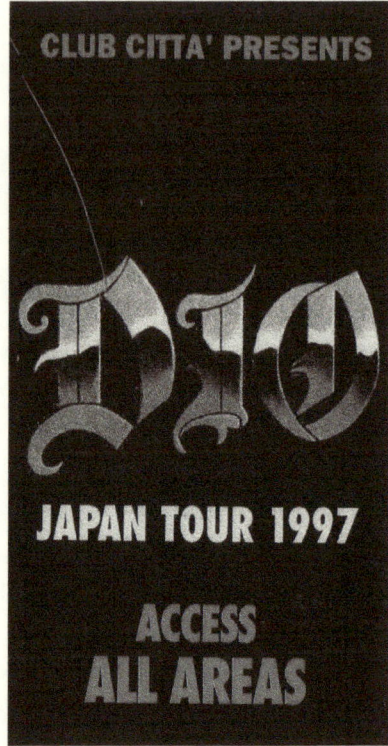

THE SONGS

This chapter is strictly about the music that Tracy made while in DIO and a song-by-song break as to putting the songs together and other thoughts about the songs from Tracy. We will start with "Strange Highways" and go all the way through to the end of the "Angry Machines" release.

"Jesus, Mary & the Holy Ghost"

Love this one. I just started jamming this riff; Pilson and Vinnie came in and jammed along.. It was a very natural song I think. Ronnie wanted something different with the verse so I hit the E diminished chord and we all said ya. Awesome tune I think. It was maybe the sixth song we wrote.

"Firehead"

It is a strange song; but very cool. I love it. It has cool lyrics too. It has a few parts. We did not play it live to much, maybe a few times. I played the main riff and it took off from there.

"Strange Highways"

I think Jeff played the main riff and I had this mellow intro part so we fused them together. Stunning heavy song with a few parts. Very cool overall. Some backwards Beatle things in the bridge. Just big, slow, mean and heavy. Ronnie's voice and Vinnie's playing are truly perfect..

"Hollywood Black"

I had that riff for years. Back in '84 I played it in a band I was part of called Swiftkick. Another one that as soon as I played it Vinnie jumped in and Ronnie was on bass for that one while we were writing it as Bain had gone and we had not yet found Pilson. Pure awesome groove, played it half the time live.

"Evilution"

One of my favorites. No solo in this one just sounds. I love it because not that many people do just sounds, they think oh I have to hit as many notes as I can. That's cool but I hear other stuff in my head sometimes and for this one it was a delay at the intro with a pterodactyl zooming in and the groove rips your balls off. Great job by everyone, great lyrics. It was a constant in the live set my entire time in the band.

"Pain"

My favorite of the entire release. It's Dio at his best. Simple heavy riff with the world's greatest rock vocalist and Vinnie the king of meat and potatoes on drums. Jimmy was on bass at first then Ronnie took over until Jeff got there. I had the riff since '89 and it fucking rocks. We played it most of the time live.

"One Foot in the Grave"

A cool song. One of the first songs we wrote. I had the main riff already. I love this song. The solo and ending were my favorite parts. I loved the cool sounds at the end. We never did play this one live.

"Give Her the Gun"

Played this one live a little bit. An absolutely beautiful song. Ronnie let me use his 12-string for the intro which was very cool. Great vocals and lyrics. Ronnie could sing anything.

"Blood from a Stone"

I had the riff already. The song had a great groove and sadly we never played it live.

"Here's to You"

We played live a bit but not my favorite song. At one point Ronnie said we need an up-tempo tune. So what you hear is what came out. It was a natural feel to me. It was forced to a point. I wished we just did another mid-tempo tune with balls but Ronnie did not want all the songs to be the same tempo which I understand. It just seemed a little forced to me.

"Bring Down the Rain"

We never played it live and that is too bad as it is an awesome song. I had the riff sitting around for three years. Heavy yet melodic with heavy vocals; great song I think.

"Angry Machines"

"Institutional Man"

One of the first songs written for the project. Too many parts in the song I think but some cool parts. Ronnie was not sure what to sing over the 5/8 part and it was strange for a Dio song to play in a time other than 4/4 but how cool and I loved it. My favorite part was when Vinnie told Ronnie not too follow us but just sing over the top and he did. People might not get it and I am so sorry but we loved it. We only played it a few times live.

"Don't Tell the Kids"

I had the main riff already but again the song was broken up into too many parts I think and it just did not flow like a song should. Some cool parts again but I never was happy with the outcome. We never played it live.

"Black"

Awesome song with an awesome but jacked-up chord that is not normal sounding but loved it. Again I feel like it is just to different to the normal Dio fan in Whoville. Great vocals and lyrics with an awesome groove. Only played a few times live.

"Hunter of the Heart"

Hanging out at Ronnie's house and went into his home studio and played the riff. He really liked it so we demoed it with the drum machine then took it to practice for everyone else to hear. I liked this one a lot and it has a great groove to it. Played it the whole AM tour and Inferno tour.

"Stay Out of My Mind"

A full Jeff Pilson song and a good song. We pretty much just learned it from his demo and played it like he wanted it. Ronnie did not write the lyrics and I did not write any music. Ronnie worked on the keyboard solo with Scott in the middle of the song. Not a big fan of keyboard solos. Never played it live.

"Big Sister"

Killer tune, killer groove. Played it live a few times. Absolutely loved the song; it is big and heavy and great lyrics.

"Double Monday"

Played it live a lot. I had the riff already in my back of riffs. Ended up being another strange one but it was cool I think. Kinda up-tempo but sounded natural to me. Cool words.

"Golden Rules"

Loved the groove. The guitar rhythm over the verse is so cool. Nice spooky intro like a twisted little kid song. Love it but never played it live.

"Dying in America"

Another strange but awesome song. Most of this stuff just did not sit right with the diehard Dio fans, just too different for their brains. Bummer because there are some cool parts on this whole CD.

"God Hates Heavy Metal" (Bonus Track)

Jerry Best played bass in the first part of the AM sessions and he wrote this riff and we all wrote the rest of it around the riff. Very cool riff. Never played it live and it only came out on the Japanese release.

"This is Your Life"

Stunning and beautiful. A friend Dave Cevantez made a few guitars for me and the main part and verse of the song was born from the baritone guitar he made. It was tuned to low B so when I cleaned up the sound and played a simple chord like a C chord it was stunning, sad and moody. It was both dark and beautiful. It was all baritone guitar and strings and a little drums at first, but when Ronnie was tracking it in the studio he changed it to all piano and him singing. Either way it speaks for itself and Ronnie's voice is soulful and stunning. Never played it live. It was tough to play a lot of "AM" songs live because I think they did not flow so good and did not feel good live. Maybe thats why a lot of people did not get this body of work. It was a tough time for whatever reason and the CD reflects that but I still dig it.

THE DIO YEARS DISCOGRAPHY

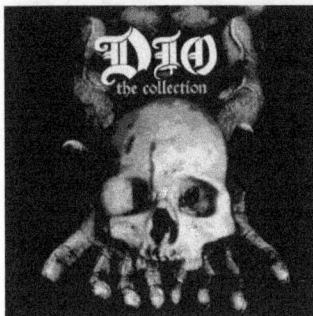

G. GEAR

What do you say about gear that people will understand universally? To a guitar player who takes their craft and what they do seriously gear is the equivalent to KISS and their make up, a plumber and his wrenches, a graphic artist and their computer, a girl with her purse and an addict with their fix.

Gear is what drives the brain to come up with the things it does. This is no different from any other profession in reality it just has different components that make it all up.

From the mid 1980s Tracy started building his arsenal that really has not changed but very little to this day. Many players will adapt with the times or try to stay up to date with the latest and greatest product. G is not one of those guys. What he has is what he has and no one can use it like he does. It is not that Tracy has anything so different from many other players out there but there is no doubt that he uses it in a way that no one else has thought of that is for sure.

Tracy is not one for trading in anything either. Most of this gear was present even before DIO but it was all brought into the DIO fold and not without some eye brows being raised. His gear has been all around the world. It has sweated and it has froze but the one thing is for sure; when it is time to play rock and roll it has always done its job.

Now lets first take a look at the amplification that Tracy used during the DIO days. What great guitar player in this heavy genre of music does not use or has not used a Marshall cabinet? Tracy supported (6) 4x12 cabinets. While on tour he always used Ronnie's cabinets but used his own for studio and rehearsals. Tracy's cabinets are all powered with 25-watt greenback celestions. This is another reason for that great tone. Most standard Marshall cabinets come from the plant with 75-watt speaker in them. By dropping the 75 to 25 you are creating a speaker that will break up better under the massive amount of power being shoved into it by the 100-watt Marshall. The average person or weekend guitarist out there will never know how important that speaker is to the overall tone of the player on the other end of the cable.

Now his live set up for actual power was the same on the road and the studio except for the "Angry Machines" sessions. That is the only time Tracy ever recorded with one cabinet in Mono and used one Randall head only. Tracy used (1) Marshall 1970 100-watt head, (1) 50-watt Marshall head and (3) Randall RG-80 solid state heads. All of this was configured to run stereo both in the studio and for live. G used all of his own gear for the entire "Strange Highways" world tour. In Europe for "Angry Machines" however the heads differed as the gear was provided on most touring there. The unique combination of the solid state Randall and classic Marshall 1970s heads help deliver that powerful kick in the teeth that Tracy has become known for. It also helped in the original tone he developed that helped define the Dio sound of the 90's and was sorely missed after he left.

It was obvious from hearing the initial notes of the Strange Highways release that the guitar tone was so much bigger than that of any other DIO release or any related Ronnie James Dio project before it. Iommi always had a big sound but it was never this defined and tight and did not have as much punch either. It was much bigger than that of any of the previous guitarist that were in Dio. It was just totally removed and beyond what had come before it and as I was told by Ronnie personally; "no one has ever been able to replicate his tone since." He also went on to tell me that no one could get the playing he did right either and that was one reason why none of the Tracy G stuff was played live after he left with the exception of the 1999 Eurofest tour where Craig Goldy attempted it with no success at all.

Tracy also ran a rack mount effects set up. This set up is not so different from what many players use on the circuit today. G ran (1) Lexicon 41 Delay/Chorus, (1) Lexicon Alex Delay, (1) Boss DE-200 and (1) MXR Delay 200. This is not to say that everyone uses the same rack mount effects but the style of effects be it delay, chorus, verb, etc., are used by many in their chain.

In this chain of mayhem that Tracy has created is Igor - the pedal board. This pedal board was given its name by the great Ronnie James Dio. At one of the rehearsals for the first world tour Tracy was told by an assistant of Ronnie's that he would need to get a new board. Tracy responded by saying that the band would just need to get a new guitarist then because that is his pedal board and that was how he would roll. Once you look at the picture of this pedal board in this chapter one will see why Ronnie gave it the name he did.

It is not a pretty sight by any means but the key to it very simple. Tracy created it, placements, wiring, tape and all but it was part of his being so to speak. Ronnie was used to seeing neat and clean-looking pedal boards with all the players he had been on the road with but it was clear Tracy was changing all of that. So in response Ronnie had a case built for the pedal board and G took it on the road for six years around the world while in DIO.

The pedal board is made up of (1) Boss Volume Pedal, (1) Boss Noise gate, (1) Fultone Octafuzz, (1) A.D.A Flanger and

(1) Boss tuner. On top of that you have a ton of wires and tape to make up Igor.

Everything about what Tracy had and used help make him the unique player that he is today and was while in DIO. Let's face it; Tracy was way ahead of his time in the 90's and whether you got it then or are just now getting it today it has made him stand above the rest.

Tracy was also unique that his guitars were not store bought guitars. His main axe for the DIO years was made by Karl Sandoval. The very same Karl Sandoval that made the infamous Randy Rhoads' polka-dotted Flying V along with guitars for Eddie Van Halen, George Lynch and the list goes on. Tracy had known Karl for quite a while because he worked for him at his store.

One day Karl told G that it was time to make a guitar for him. Tracy was floored by this. A guitar of his own, in his own style and look. When they went to the wood store to pick out a piece of wood to make the guitar out of Tracy floored his boss by what he picked out. While Karl was looking at the wood he was asked to come over to a dumpster by G. He had found a piece of wood that was assumed to be left over scrap or not usable. Sandoval thought Tracy was out of his mind but G did not want the glossy sleek look that guitars players were looking for then. He wanted it to look different and this piece of wood was just that from the driftwood appearance to the knots in the wood. Karl said OK and took that wood and made the guitar that has been Grijalva's main guitar since it was finished. The guitar was molded from a Stratocaster style, but, its look was totally its own.

Tracy also as a back up had a Black Custom Strat that Sandoval made for his as well. In 1995, Tracy had David Cervantes build him a couple more guitars in the holy guitar look. Dave also over time became G's guitar tech by both building and setting up his guitars for studio and the road. Dave also built the baritone guitar that Tracy was wanting to use on the "Angry Machines" release that was not received as hoped by DIO. That guitar however would go on and do some amazing work for Grijalva in his post DIO work.

For "Strange Highways," Grijalva used only his holy custom Strat. On "Angry Machines" however he brought in the baritone guitar for "This is My Life" and he also used his 1975 Gibson Explorer on a few songs for both rhythms and solos.

For the most part all the gear used looks old, is old, beaten-up and rough-looking. That is the way Tracy likes it to be. He compares it to an old pair of jeans that have been broken in and just fit right. In many ways that is totally the way it should be and let's face it; if it fits great it performs great.

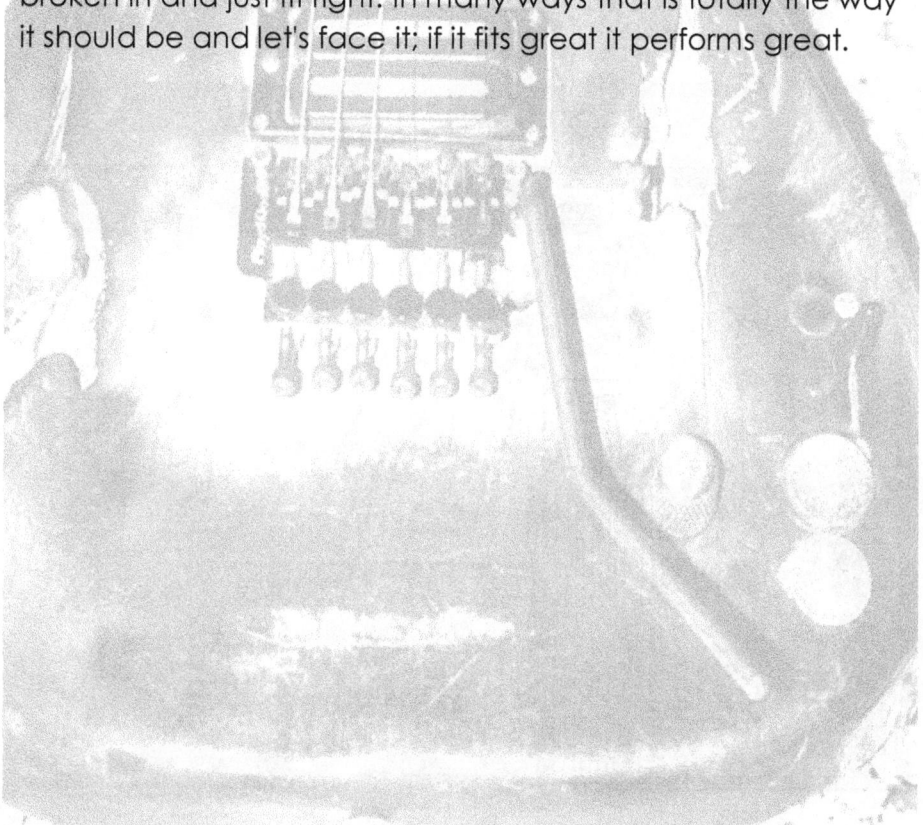

IGOR 1993

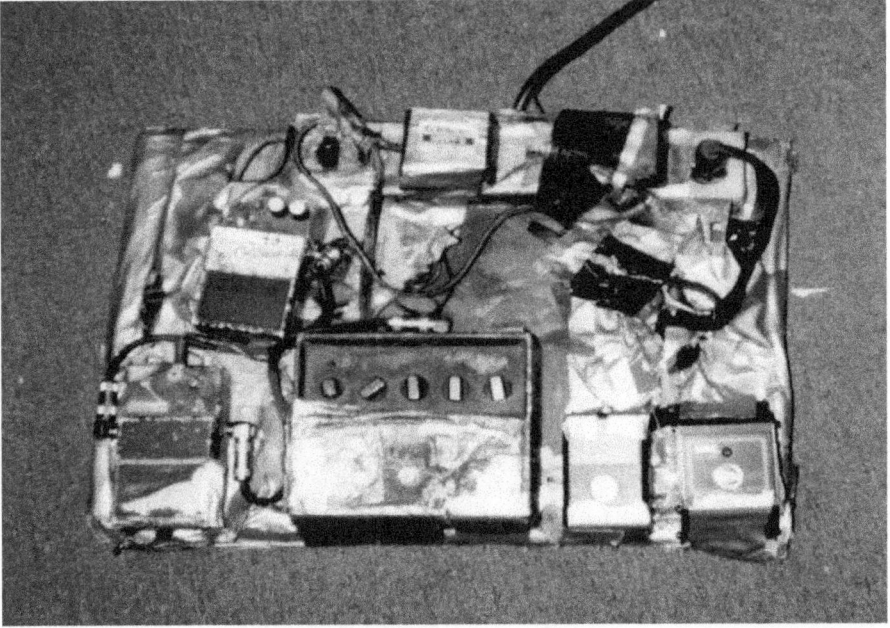

IGOR In Road Case

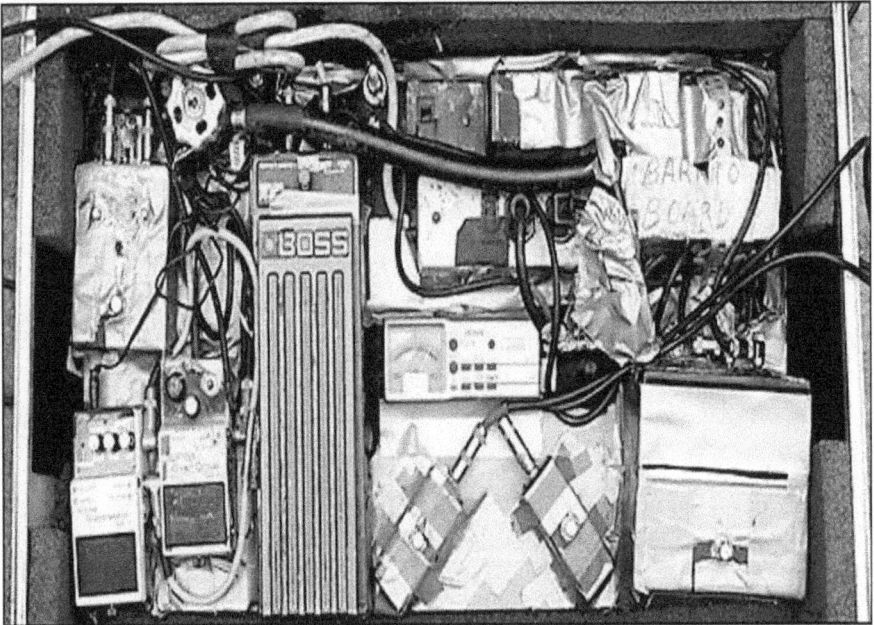

IGOR 2012

The Holy Guitar

The Power

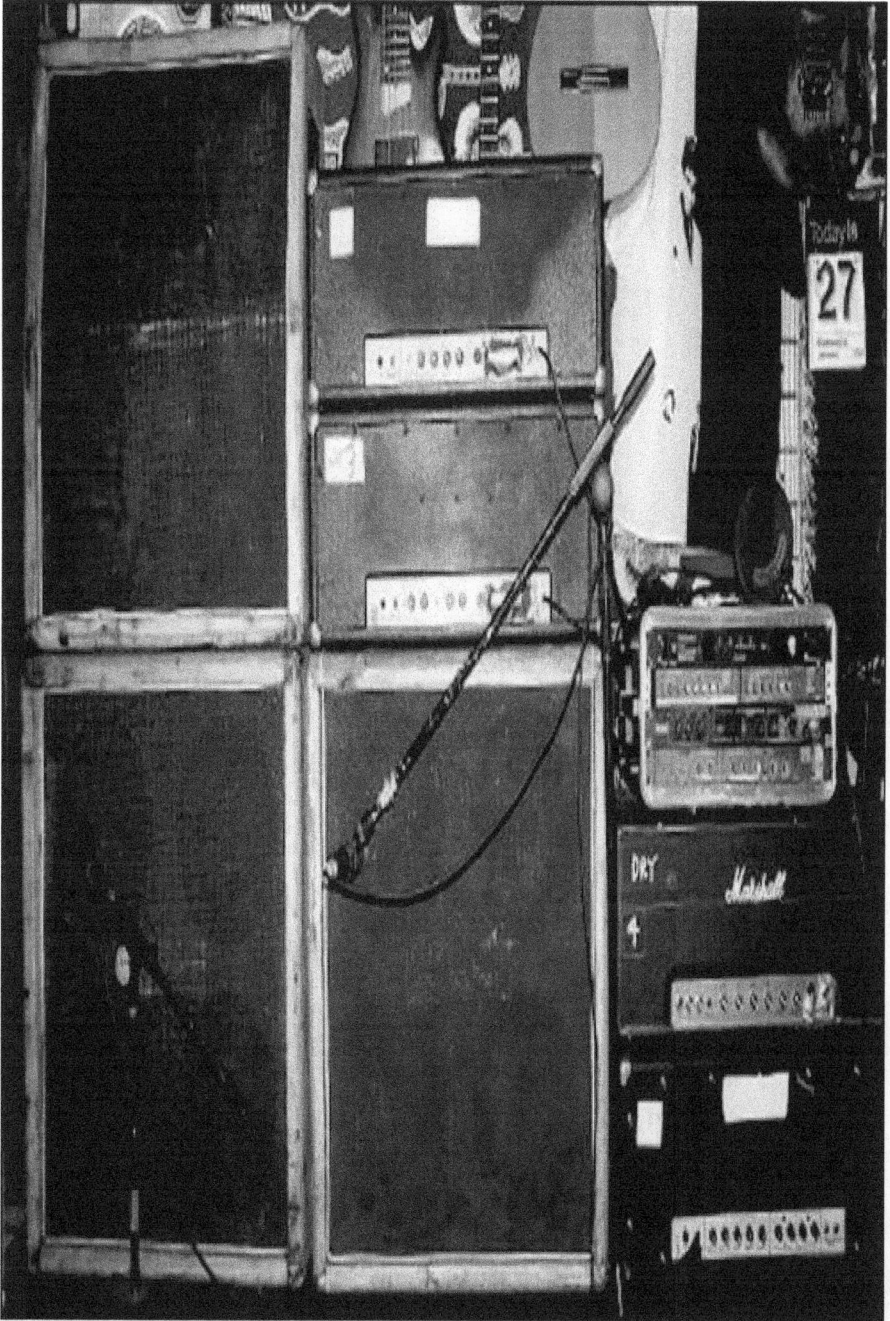

Holy Guitar #2

Rack Mount Gear

The G Man

Musical Spaghetti

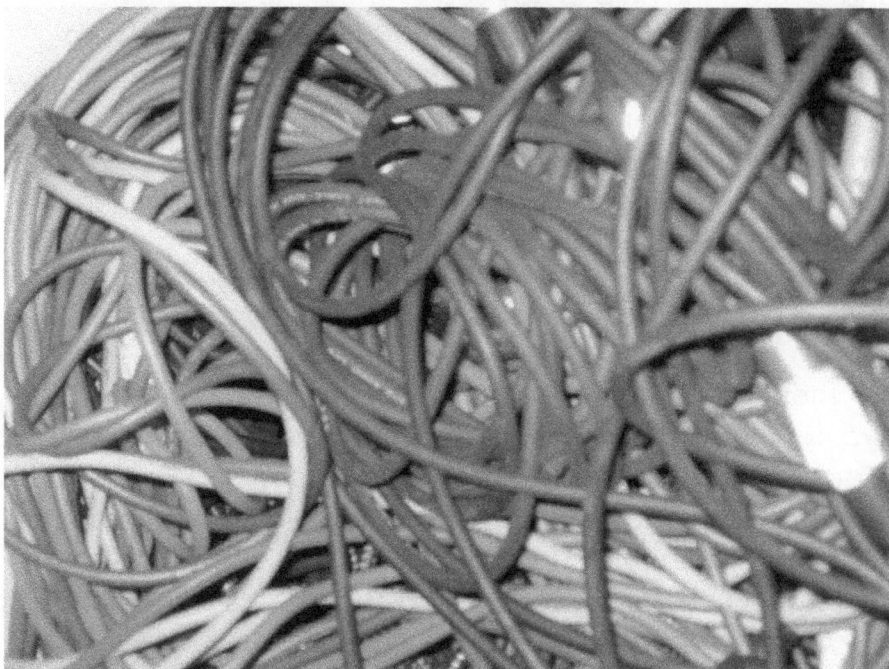

BEYOND THE SKULL

Since his departure from DIO in 1999, Tracy has been a continued fountain of creative fire. There have been a total of 25 releases made by Tracy in various formats, genres and line-ups.

The one thing you cannot do is judge his time in DIO as the only thing defines this great virtuoso. Yes, he is a heavy player by nature but his music is colored with many flavors and just about everything that is out there in music.

Right after the Dio departure Tracy wanted to do something ultra heavy and use some of those riffs that were passed on in the "Angry Machines" sessions. So he went out and enlisted the help of Ray Luzier who is the drummer of Korn. He then went into the G. Factory Studio and created along with Luzier and singer Tim Saxton a band called Driven. This was totally seen as a way to get the aggression out and show what he was all about in a metal kind of way. G also knew that trying to find a singer that was in the same vein as Ronnie would not work nor would it look good so he sat out to find someone with a lot of angst and anger in their approach and that was Tim Saxton.

They would go in and craft a four-song ball burner called "Work in Process." That would grow from that EP to a full-on release called "Citizen X" later the same year of 1999. It was plain and simple with no sugar coating to this band. They wanted to find you; pound you into submission and then go hunt down the next person and do more of the same. This was before Lamb of God and bands like that but the blue print was there.

Tracy wanted to show everyone what he was all about and there was no doubt after these two releases that he was not playing around and was a serious contender for one of the best heavy guitar players of all time.

The year 2000 saw yet another different kind of G in a different kind of lineup with a harmonica and sax in the line up of Mark Bramlett's band. He was going to play whatever he wanted as long as it was something he believed in. All the while he was producing and sharpening his skills in that area as well. Tracy also did his most mellow project with friend singer song writer Mike Beatty for a CD called me myself and the rain. 2000 also saw Driven rear its heavy head again with a promotional release. This time G brought in ex-Dio bassist Larry Dennison for those duties to help free him up for the production and to concentrate just on the guitar duties.

The next year, 2001 saw G release the first of two Christmas products. 2001 saw "A Spooky G XMas" make its way out of the G Factory on the Spooky G label. Also that year there was a lighter release called "Katt Gutt." But notably Driven was back again for their first big release on MTM records called "Self Inflicted." This was a 12-song opus that was intense from note one. This release seriously had the intense power that could hurt a person just by listening to it. This release along with all the Driven releases are so powerful and intense that Tracy and I have decided to rerelease the best of them all for everyone to hear.

This was a release that really made an impact on the brain. Tracy was at his brutal best on this album and he was also letting go of some frustration as well. The one thing to be noted about this is that a lot of the material came from riffs that were passed on during the "Angry Machine" sessions while in DIO. The Lineup had G, Saxton, Dennison and Mike Terrana.

Also as of this writing G has rereleased Goad-ed's " To Die is Gain" CD. This is another truly heavy groovin' masterpiece. This lineup of Ruzier, G, Dennison and new singer Jason Witte truly were clicking on all cylinders for this epic collection of tunes.

Throughout the years Tracy has gone on to release any thing from a covers CD to a Spanish release of beautiful nylon string arrangements and a full-on instrumental release as well. This axemaster has proven time and time again that he is a great player and not only that he has such an understanding of what is need to make a song great regardless of the genre.

From a kid who was told that his hands were to small at the age of seven to play a guitar to the man who sat in one of the driver's seats in the world of rock as a player in Dio he has proven himself repeatedly. The guy is pure genius in his approach to playing and writing music.

His vision has always been very clear from day to one. "I have to do it and do it my way." That is all he has ever known and he was never in the early days going to compromise his beliefs and what he wanted just like he wasn't going to in DIO or his own thing he has going on to this very day.

It is not that G wanted out of Dio but he just did not share the vision that was being laid down. Tracy loved playing music with the biggest voice in the business but the change that Dio was undertaking was not in the picture for what he would see himself doing in the future. He wanted to continue to make fresh exciting heavy music and not regress to a golden age that had long since been overtaken in the scene.

In the six years of being in DIO Tracy helped produce three releases. Those releases were marked by innovative writing, playing and touring in support of them. His guitar style brought a new edge to a classic band and gave it some much needed teeth. He gave Ronnie James Dio the sound that his voice always needed and deserved inside of the DIO band. Never ever for any reason sacrificing his own integrity as a player and how he envisioned the way it could and should be.

These things have not changed to this day and I have a good reason to believe that they never will with Tracy either. He stands rock solid in his belief, his style and his approach to his love in life - playing the guitar and making music. That, dedication and dogged determination in itself deserves the highest level of respect one can get.

If you are a fan of Tracy G then you know all about what he has done since 1999. If you are a casual fan and had no idea I urge you to go to his official web site which is simply (www.tracyg.com) and get hooked up with some of the fabulous releases he has put out since the Dio days.

Unlike so many of his contemporaries who sit around and wait for a chance in a big-name act Tracy will never be that guy. He has gone out and stood on his own for many reasons of which are all his own. G makes "G music" with no give and take involved - playing just what he feels in his gut. That is why you see 25 releases in the past 12 years. A musician is supposed to have something to say and so many just really do not. They sit around waiting for the big money or that awesome run of dates for the lime light. Don't get me wrong; Tracy is not allergic to that either but he simply plays music because it is his love and his passion and that's what he was put here on the earth to do.

He is alive and well and making some of the best heavy ass-kicking music on the planet still in his Tracy G group with Johnny B on drums and vocals and Eddie Frisco on bass. The TGG just released "Controlled Chaos" and are already at work on the next product and playing live as well. Tracy G - a true musician and brilliant tactician and nowhere near being done with his message.

Sure it's been a long, trip on a 'strange highway,' but the real road and a horizon with a burning sun lies ahead. It is now just getting interesting!

Anyone who knows Grijalva knows that he is anything but the rock star type. He just is not a guy who has the attitude that we have come to know through people who we won't mention here. His feeling is very simple and that is just to be a good person and do what it is you were put here to do and don't be a dick in the process.

One of the very first things I picked up on about Tracy is the fact that he is a down-to-earth person who just loves his family, friends and what he does. He is very easy to talk to and with. For those fans who do not know much about this guy personally he is the ultimate funny guy. His guitar playing is matched only by his incredible sense of humor.

Tracy wants to leave this collection of history that he has created by saying a few words about the man who put him in the position to be able to create these memories.

"When I was 15 Gibert H - a friend of mine - let me hear "Man on the Silver Mountain" by Ritchie Blackmore's Rainbow. I remember being blown away by the voice in the song finding out that voices name was Ronnie Dio. From that moment on I was a giant fan of his voice and never thought I would meet him let alone be the guitar player and write music with him in his band someday. It was truly an amazing time for me. Ronnie James Dio might be gone now but his music and voice will out live us all. To one of the best rock vocalist to ever live; Long live Ronnie James Dio and thanks for the ride."

This entire process while working on this book with Tracy has been amazing for me to be sure. I would like to thank Tracy G and his sister Shawn and their family for the gifts and help to finish this book. I would also like to thank my wife Julie for always being the support I need to accomplish whatever I want.

In closing Tracy would like to leave thanks as well:

"I would like to thank the following people: Jeff and Julie Westlake, Mom, Dad, Shawn, Toni, Taylor, Britt, Mark Caro, Jim Montoya, Paul Hunder, Adam Weber with one fucking B, Julie P. Hand, Johnny B, Eddie Frisco,Ray Luzier, Chris Koeng, Rob Domingues at Grayspace Design, Paul and Wendy Alfrey, Paul the Rog Rogne from Metalkast, Mike Beatty, Ron Lira, Jim Reyes, Gordon Lug Nutz Stewart, Jim, Tina, Jake and Josh Jones (The skull lives), Creep Factory, Dave Banks, Dominic and Suzy Chavez, Paul Saghera, Johnny Bug and Kathy, Ruben Marron, Rudy Ram Rod Torrez and family, Vito Racano, Allen from the Right To Rock, Angel Cruchett, Larry Ramirez at D.O.B., Ed Cota, Gratz, Barbara Shore, Mike Kearns, Steve at Brazen Guitars, Allen Lane and all the Dio and Tracy G fans."

WORDS THAT MATTER

"This is the best the Dio band ever sounded. Tracy is the guitar player that Dio should of always had. Jeff Pilson is the bass player that Dio should of always had. Luckily Vinny and I stayed together through it all. This album the band is playing great. It is more focused on what we were doing and what we wanted to be. Years from now somebody is going to say where is all the good music? Well, let them here this one and they will remember." **Ronnie James Dio** on Strange Highways

"I can remember a period in rock history in the early 90s where everything changed. Most of the notable artists from the previous decades were faced with challenges thatwould leave some to perish with dying careers, and propel others to new heights. Around this time, I thought of many of the artists who had influenced me as a musician most notably, the heavy metal artists. Who will survive the test of time with this new face of music? One artist that came to mind that I never wanted to see fade into black was Ronnie James Dio. His last album before the big change was, Lock Up The Wolves, which was a really good album, but I knew he had much more to say. Surprisingly, Ronnie emerged with a new guitarist named Tracy Grijalva, or as the fans knew him as Tracy G, with two new studio records, Strange Highways and Angry Machines. A raw, compositional injection of powerful guitar riffs, structures, and tone brought an innovativeness to the new music of Dio that had not been witnessed since Ronnie's days with Rainbow and Black Sabbath, and would also result in the induction of a whole new generation of fans with the old. I would soon learn more about the diversity of this guitarist that makes him, to this day, a stand-alone compared to many other players in the industry, and continues to define his musical endeavors as nothing less than brilliant." **Jeff Boggs** - Hydrogyn-Ura-Kia

The unorthodox and outside the box guitar playing style of TracyG, along with the way with words and sheer powerful vocals of Ronnie James Dio are magic, as featured on the incomparable Strange Highways, CD. **Jimmy Montoya**.

"Tracy G, is normally a fairly hard core guitar player. His years in Dio, and other projects, all bare that out, but this CD was a complete departure for him. Having the pleasent task of Mastering this CD, I had to listen to it for quite a period. It was excellently recorded, and played mainly all by Tracy himself. His talent just jumps out at you, when listening to this CD. Even if this type of music, is not normally your 'cup of tea', you will appreciate the talent required, and the recording itself. I've known Tracy for several years, and I'm still amazed when listening to this CD. Pick it up! You will NOT be disappointed!" **Scot Clyaton** - SMC Productions

"Tracy G. stepped up to the spotlight and delivered a guitar solo that reached into your soul and literally ripped it apart. Everyone in the crowd was just floored! The notes that he hit were mind-shattering! Tracy G.'s guitar must have set off the movement detectors at Cal Poly for sure!" Tony Sisson Angry Machines tour "in my opinion, today's Dio couldn't have any better guitarist! His playing fits perfectly in Dios current musical style and he can play the old songs as well, no matter what people say." **Tapio Keihänen** Angry Machines Tour

"After the show my friend praised Tracy's solo for the huge range of expression in various feelings. Also said to me, "From the first line to the last one all the audience raised their fists and totally united." Yoko Nakajima (Japan) Angry Machines Tour "Moreover what I want to write especially is that guitar solo was very attractive. I think Tracy seemed to take emotional feelings partially and it successfully adds a little gentle feelings to his originally abstract, philosophical and aggressive feelins. His solo comes just after two old tunes above mentioned. This stream is really artistic. Every time I listen to his guitar, I like his attitudes and music sense more and more." Yoko Nakajima (Japan) Angry Machines Tour "Strange Highways" is the heaviest and arguably the angriest album in Dio's long solo career. I did not like it that much at first, because it was a great departure from his previous albums, containing darker lyrical themes and noticeably heavier music. However, it slowly grew on me, and it now stands as my favorite Dio album ever, with not a weak song on it. Fan Review by, **Shaft** .

"This release features a darker, almost angrier Dio. I have been a Jeff Pilson fan for quite a while from his Dokken days. One of the things that always disappointed me about the Dokken recordings was that it was very difficult to hear Pilson's bass. Not on this one...the sound is great! Tracy G's guitar is hard and rips like a chain saw, The CD is solid and worthy to be a part of any head banger's library." Fan Review

"Strange Highways and Holy Diver are the best Dio albums by far. There will always be a certain contingent of Dio fans who hate Strange Highways for reasons unkown to me, though most site Tracy G. However, Mr. G is one of those guitarist - like a young Tony Iommi - who obviously sold his soul for Rock and Roll! His riffs are satanic - in the good way. Thank God RJD didn't try to put another sackless "virtuoso" like the crapmaster from Lock up the Wolves on this album. Tracy G has the most in your face solos since Vivian. Sure he doesn't play at high velocity but who cares? It is the spirit that matters.

Not buying in? Then ask yourself: who is cooler Hendrix or Yngwie? I rest my case. It always pains me to think that a small vocal minority - the D and D variety of Dio fans - bitched so much about Strange Highways that he totally changed his direction. This Orson-Scott-Cardesque stuff of the last several years is anything but magic no matter how many references he makes to conjuring wizards. I am a grown man. I do not want a Dio album with topics best suited for anime or T-shirts with dragons. I want Firehead blaring from my speakers and that freak monster on the cover of the album on a a black shirt - hell maybe even tatooed on my nuts. Yes, the album is that good. Buy this album if you like RJD and you will see that if you tear yourself away from nostalgia, this is his greatest recording." **S. Roy** - Fan Review

"I had heard this was like Strange Highways and, since that is a great album, I had to get this one. While this is not the same sound as Strange Highways, it is equally heavy. I have always enjoyed Holy Diver and Last in Line, but I felt there were some weaknesses in his ensuing albums (Sacred Heart and Dream Evil) with too many weak filler songs and too much synthesizer even on the better tracks. I love the dark, heavy stuff Dio does like Strange Highways and his Sabbath/Heaven and Hell albums. This album is in that same vein and is hard driving and extremely heavy...Tracy G. rocks on lead guitar! It has a bunch of outstanding, catchy songs on it (Institutional Man, Hunter of the Heart, Dying in America, Double Monday, Don't Tell the Kids, Black, and Stay Out of My Mind). There is certainly no light and/or overly synthesized stuff on here, save for the light final track (This Is Your Life). It took me a few listens to get into it, but once I did, it was well worth it. Dio took a chance with this and, Imo, it paid off huge! I would recommend it to both Dio fans and fans of heavy metal looking for something new." **Old School Metal Review**

"People were complaining about Killing the Dragon and Master of the Moon being too repetitive--do you know why? Because when Dio tries to do something new and different, like this album, the fans hate it! I saw a review down there somewhere, a very short one: "PIANOS??? WTF THIS ISN'T DIO!" or something along those lines. But the more open-minded fans out there will probably enjoy this. Of course it's really not anything like Holy Diver etc, but you have to admit this is some pretty intelligent music! ANGRY MACHINES sees Dio experimenting a bit with odd time signatures (Double Monday or Dying in America for example) and new sounds. Tracy G's guitar style is very unique, I love how he uses those strange intervals (b5's mostly, for musicians who might be reading,) to create a really evil-sounding riff, with the occasional shred thrown in. And lyrically the album is actually better than the "classics," I'd say. Rather than demons and wizards etc, Angry Machines mostly deals with the problems of society today. The lyrics to "Dying in America" are probably some of the best I've heard! And as far as the music itself, I don't know why so many people dislike this album. The songs are catchy and heavier than before as well. Personal favorites include Dying in America, Hunter of the Heart (live version is awesome,) and Double Monday (I love the interlude!) Hard-rocking and well thought-out songs, both musically and lyrically. Most importantly, it's different from the other albums! And if you're a Dio fan, isn't that worth buying it for already?" Fan review by **NoSoup4you**

"Tracy G. is a rare individual/Musician who is Driven, dynamic, professional, passionate, respectful, and has a lot of class. He has a unique one-of-a-kind playing style that can be powerful, beautiful, haunting, mysterious, and more. He plays with a lot of emotion that comes from within and afar.And to top it off : he is the same person no matter if he has played in front of 20 or 20,000 people - and he Has Rocked them all..

Anyone who seen the DIO Strange Highways / Angry Machines tours knows what I am talking about...... His years in Dio showed that he is in the same league as every Guitar player that Ronnie James Dio has been in a Band with only the Great have played with him. I am honored and thankful to have recorded with Tracy and known him all these years. All the Best indeed." **Rucker Kelly**

"After Dio's "Doom Broom" was implemented in 1990 I was very interested in seeing where Jimmy Bain & Vinny Appice would end up. With the debut release of WWIII in 1991 I was reacquainted with not only what I considered the best rhythm section this side of metal, but the guitar styling of Tracy G. I was immediately hooked on his wall of sound and diminished chords. After seeing the band I was fortunate to meet them all and I remember thinking as awesome it was to meet my idol Jimmy Bain, it was Tracy that really blew me away with his kindness.

Flash forward to the Dio press release in 1993 announcing the new line up that included Tracy G. Man, was I one happy f*cker. I knew DIO were gonna have balls and I knew Ronnie found himself another talented musician that had heart. From the barrage of sound that opens "Jesus, Mary & The Holy Ghost" to the haunting chords in "Evilution" to the 'not so ballad' ballad "Give Her The Gun", I knew I was right to be a Tracy G fan.

It was on the "Strange Highways", Angry Machines" and "Dio's Inferno-Last In Live" tours that Tracy and I solidified our friendship. Seeing Dio perform over 50 shows on these three tours I spent a lot of time with Tracy. We spoke of gear, the music industry, his time with Dio & he was pivotal in helping my band open for Dio by talking to Ronnie after hearing our demo. But I recall even more fondly our personal & candid chats...He treated me as if I were a friend and know full well

133

that I am. "Here's To You" Tracy G!!!!" **Jim Hoefelt A.K.A. "BIG Jim"**

Talk about the era of Tracy with DIO: To sum up the year's of DIO with Tracy G, it was the only time that DIO's sound was truly dark. Tracy's screeching intro set the tone of Strange Highways that quickly moved the listener to some of the heaviest and most guttural guitar riff's ever expressed on an Instrument. This music was equally matched by the only vocalist on the planet that couldsing to such a sound; Ronnie James DIO. Strange Highway's ushered in a new chapter in DIO's career, the music was so dark at times it scared people.

Frankly, I will never understand why there was such a DIO fan backlash with Tracy'splaying, this is the first time I really started listening to DIO and it was because ofTracy's playing, it was different, edgy, and dangerous, and DIO finally had a sound thatmatched his mystical, dark persona.

It's also important to note that Dio defended Tracy in interviews until Dios death, he fully believed in Tracy. Dio has called Tracy one of the most innovative and inspiring guitarists he has EVER worked with and that people should respect him for that. It's a shame that Dio caved to pier pressure, one can only imagine what would have been created if Dio would have stuck with what he wanted to do.

People have to remember that when Strange Highways was released grunge was raising its ugly head and most people were hanging onto the 80's to a point where they wanted music familiarity. Rob Zombie, Marilyn Manson, and the new era of darker sounding metal was just starting to build, Strange Highways is a record that was truly ahead of its time! Ironically, 80's Dio fan's that I introduce to Strange

Highways today, a record they refused to listen to in the past, often times becomes one of their top Dio releases.

Talk about Tracy as a player:

Tracy eats, breaths and shit's the guitar, the guitar is a true extension of who he is as a person. Music allows Tracy to convey emotions that he has inside that he can't express in any other way; he can do this through music alone, without words. As accomplished a guitar player that Tracy is, like a great musician, it's the emotion of the song and the moment that sells his music. Tracy said to me many times "if I hit a note, hold that note, and that note is the whole solo, it's there because it means something". While most players are trying to write the next hit, Tracy is creating and exploring the guitar and how it communicates through music.

Tracy's sound, his sound and style is as unique as Eddie Van Halen's is, and as important in my opinion. He is one of the few musician's in history that has created his own signature sound and he has the conviction to follow that exploration whether it be a riff, picking techniques, he has mastered the use of the tritone (The Devils Chord), and more importantly; his sounds.

To help create his sound Tracy has customize guitars that are often as unconventional as his known playing. His customized guitar of choice has been Sandoval guitars with

custom pick up's, heavy gauge strings. He often burns his guitar, cut's it, smashes it, and chops into the look and feel he wants for that guitar. Before baritone guitars were a fad, Tracy built his own, he called me and said "dude check this out, it's sick"; it was the meanest guitar sound I had heard.

Igor; his pedal board, was named by Dio, it is the most unique efx pedal set up I've ever seen. Most guitarist's try to make their pedal set up look as pretty and as clean as possible, not Tracy, it looks like it's from hell. He's got knobs, screwed onto this thing that has traveled the world many time's over and upon first site you may think that it's couldn't survive a trip to the curb. It's his unique use of these pedals and efx that help him to create these monstrous sounds that only he can do.

Because of some of his successful bands Tracy is known for his sounds and heavy thick riff's, most people don't know that he can play anything, perfectly no less. There is rarely a time when I talk with Tracy that he doesn't have a guitar strapped on, he will all of a sudden start playing a riff and ask me to guess it, most of the time it is a perfect reproduction of a riff, often Van Halen or the Beatles. His flamingo guitar playing is unparalleled and people who hear his flamingo influenced CD called Grijalva are amazed at his versatility.

Instead of me gushing about his playing lets just look at the facts, early on his playing stood out of the crowd enough to get him an audition with Ozzy that Jake E. Lee ultimately got, his first band that went national is WWIII and featured one of the greatest rhythm sections of all time, Vinnie Appice and Jimmy Bain. Although his introduction to Dio was through Vinnie, it was his playing that got him the gig with the greatest

singer of all time Ronnie James Dio! If that wasn't enough he went on to work for many

years with Ray Luzier (DLR Band, Korn, Army of Anyone) and Mike Terrana (Yngwie Malmsteen, Kuni, Tony Macalpine, Rage, Axel Rudi Pell), Jeff Pilson (Dio, Dokken), Mikkey Dee (Motorhead) to name a few.

Tracy has created some of the most incredible music I have ever heard. He continues to innovate and inspire top players and novices alike. PAUL"The Rogue"ROGNE

"Tracy G is a force of nature" **Paul Hudner**

G Quotes

" I was real excited about the call and thinking that Vinny should of made sure it happened any way ahahah." Tracy on his reaction to being asked to try out for Dio.

" I remember feeling weak all of the sudden and then pulled it together to go tell my dad I was the guitar player in Dio. "Tracy's reaction to getting the job in Dio.

" I thought I just wanna go back over the Atlantic and go home. There is no reason why I should be traveling across a body of frozen salt water. This just isn't right." The first truly cold run of dates in Europe.

" It was so surreal and I probably missed most of what was said but damn; I went from the out house to the penthouse in a blink of an eye." The thought process in Tracy's mind at the first meeting once he was in the band at Ronnie's house.

" It just sucked ass. Vinny was the ultimate drummer at that time for what I did and the Dio sound. It was a punch to the gut but as a pro you have to move on." What was felt by Tracy upon Vinny's departure from Dio in 1998.

" We all worked hard and fast to get Simon ready and he did as good a job as you could of wanted from anyone."

On bringing Simon up to speed once he took over for Appice in 98.

" I truly love Jeff Pilson and his playing, writing and just who he is but for me doing a song that was brought into the band by him with lyrics and melody in tact was just weird of Ronnie to do." The reaction to doing the track "Stay out of my Mind" from the Angry Machines CD.

" I was just glad this entire fucking thing was over and I was more than ready to go on tour." Talking about the writing for the Angry Machines CD.

" I looked in my pocket after rehearsal and saw that Ronnie handed me a check earlier. I mean damn; I actually get paid to be here too? Way too cool."

" I just immersed myself into the music right after leaving DIO and just came out with this ultra angry and aggressive music and called it Driven."

" It was fun to be able to take the old hits and fuck them all up to fit my style. Some liked it and some didn't but Ronnie never said a word to me about it."

" I asked Ronnie what he thought and he said he liked my playing alot. That was cool but I wanted to know if I had a chance so I said to him; i think my style of playing and your voice could make the coolest, heaviest, groovin Dio record ever. He just looked at me and chuckled and said.....I know exactly what you mean." Tracy's approach and question to Ronnie after try out number two.

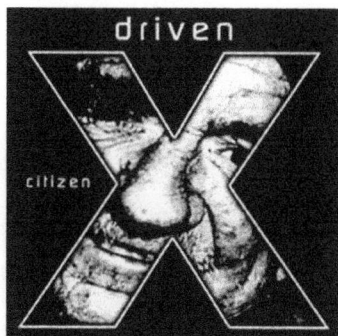

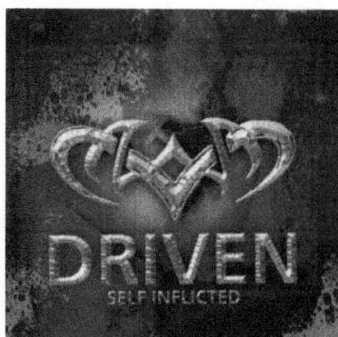

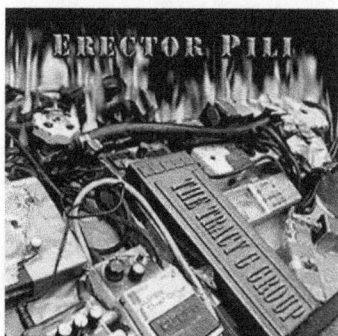

TRACY G
WWW.TRACYG.COM
WWW.MYSPACE.COM/THETRACYGGROUP

ABOUT THE AUTHOR

Jeff Westlake is an engineer, producer, guitar player and songwriter for most
of his life. Jeff has been fortunate to chart in Billboard as a producer,
engineer, writer and player multiple times throughout his career.
For over two decades now Jeff has marveled at Tracy Grijalva's playing and
mastery of the guitar. There has been a lot said and written about other
players of the Dio band era but never enough to satisfy Westlake's own
hunger to see more of it done.
This book is not only his introduction into being a writer but his take and his
homage to a player and a person that he both looks up to and now can call a
true friend.

www.ingramcontent.com/pod-product-compliance
Lightning Source LLC
Chambersburg PA
CBHW021234090426
42740CB00006B/536